Magical Elephants
And the True Meaning of Strength

By Andrew Steed

DEDICATION

This book is dedicated to my sister in Spirit, Nell-E,
who is a sprightly soul and a trusted friend and ally.
Her first name is Ellen; however, if you reverse the
letters her name becomes Nell-E. She playfully
introduced herself to me in the form of an elephant.
So thank you *'Nell-E the Elephant'* for all of the work
that you do to support me from the other side.

To the three wise elephant bulls in Kerala
who asked me to share their story:
our hearts are forever connected.

And to Snuggles and Bonnie, two pachyderms that
are faithful companions to Joyce, my partner, and
I on our travels. These two provide us with such
delight, love, and laughter and help us to stretch
our imaginations beyond the horizon!

ACKNOWLEDGEMENTS

A huge thank you to the all of the elephants who are part of this story and for their teachings on the True Meaning of Strength! I am grateful to all of the bards and storytellers who have gone before me, those who have brought the folktales, myths, and legends to my consciousness so that I can share them on in my own unique way.

I am grateful for the steadfast support of my partner and best friend, Joyce, who stands lovingly beside me in this world. It takes a team to bring a book to birth and Joyce is a key ingredient during each and every stage; she is my sounding board who helps to keep me on track and makes sure that I am well looked after as I immerse myself in the writing. Joyce's unconditional love and unwavering belief in my creativity helps to carry me through the challenges of putting myself out there in the world — thank you, it means the world to me.

Thank you to Jenna Redhawk who stepped into being my editor and has seamlessly kept the work flowing. What a star you are! Jenna told me to focus on the content and she will take care of punctuation and formatting. Wow, it has been a joy to let loose and write knowing that the nitty gritty aspects are taken care of.

Thank you for bringing your eye of Imbas to shine so diligently into all of the spaces, you are amazing!

Once again thank you, Steph Brown, for your skills and talent in designing an absolutely beautiful front and back cover worthy of carrying this book. I was tickled pink when the email came through with such a delightful cover that honours the elephants and piques the curiosity of the public to discover what's inside.

Thank you to Jennifer Fenster for sharing all of your photos of the elephants that came across your path in the wild when you were on safari in Africa. Along with the photos that I took in India, they gave Steph a strong platform to work from.

Thank you to Doron Alon for your guidance and expertise in uploading my books and for your patience in walking me through the quagmire of technology. You are a wizard at what you do.

Thank you to David Reid and Tracy Pamperin for your fine hospitality. Staying in the sanctuary of your home beside Bear Pond provided a haven that allowed the creativity to flow. And to Jan and Mike Gale for giving me the space to write in Bearspaw Canada as the moose, elk, deer, owls, crows, swans, and eagles came to see me.

Thanks to my parents Anthony John Robert Steed and Elizabeth Grace Steed who have always encouraged me to follow my dreams. To the Weegie Gang and the Fifer Gang who, along with Bonnie and Snuggles, bring so much joy into our lives.

Thanks to Pat Beck, Ryan Flannery, and Christy Davidson for standing in Battle Truth beside me in India and for gentleman George who was such a phenomenal guide.

Finally, a huge thank you to the unseen beings, my ancestral clans including the Mitchells from the Kingdom of Fife who have called me home to live in such a beautiful part of the world. To Michael Fenster for your belief, encouragement, and heartfelt friendship and to all those who have crossed paths with me who have helped shape me.

Andrew Steed has been self-employed since 1996. He has many facets to his business with the primary focus of empowering people to step into the centre of their own life stories.

PILGRIMAGES

His pilgrimages in the British Isles and Ireland offer small groups, a maximum of six people, an opportunity to expand their own horizon. These journeys allow people space to connect with their own hearts, with nature, with cultural stories, and to open up to their own creativity and authenticity through a magical adventure that is rich and rewarding.

RETREATS

He leads gatherings and retreats worldwide in the USA, Canada, Jamaica, India, Ireland, and his beloved home of the British Isles. More of his work is now offered in the UK as he looks to bring people into his back yard – especially to his ancestral lands in the Kingdom of Fife.

STORYTELLING

He is a skilled storyteller who has helped students of all ages through kindergarten to college find their voice and step into their own power in the world. He has facilitated countless residencies in schools where he has worked with children and youth for up to twenty days at a time.

LEADERSHIP TRAINING

He is an inspirational speaker whose wisdom, humour, and insight has been helping the corporate, non-profit, and educational world be more effective leaders and team players. Whether it be through a keynote address or an in-depth retreat, Andrew has helped so many beings to release, reclaim, and reweave their stories to deepen their roots and strengthen their wings.

ADDITIONAL WORKS

You can find the following titles on Amazon worldwide:

MAGICAL CROWS RAVENS AND THE CELEBRATION OF DEATH

13 STEPS TO BRINGING MAGIC INTO YOUR LIFE

POWERING UP OUR LIFE STORIES

THE FIRST SANTA

CD OF SPIRIT SONGS — SACRED OUTCAST

www.andrewsteed.com

asteed@andrewsteed.com

A COUNCIL MEETING TO DETERMINE STRENGTH

Elephant was the first to arrive. She lumbered into the clearing having bathed herself in the cool waters of the river. Feeling fresh from her cleansing she raised her trunk, jubilantly trumpeting in all of the animals who were joining the council meeting that morning.

There was a buzz in the air, for today the animals were exploring – the nature of strength.

Baboon swung effortlessly in to sit beside the pristinely groomed Cheetah. Warthog marched in and sat himself beside Crocodile who had emerged from the waters and was now basking lazily by the riverside.

Baboon fidgeted while Warthog grunted in annoyance; otherwise the five waited patiently for the arrival of Man. Man was late which wasn't unusual; however, today he was later then he had ever been before. They waited and waited and waited as the sun climbed higher until morning made way for the blistering heat of the afternoon.

When Man eventually jaunted into the circle, Warthog let out his loudest grunt for instead of an apology, Man exclaimed merrily, "Let's get cracking then! I have things to do today. Come on, chop chop! Who is going to get this show on the road? Don't all look at me, I have just run on in here and would appreciate a quick breather before dazzling you with a demonstration of mighty Man's true power and strength!" he winked at the astonished faces of the council as he flashed a polished grin from ear to ear.

The wise old sage Elephant read the situation clearly. She saw the anger bubbling on Warthog's bristles and seized the moment to diffuse a possibly explosive situation. "Warthog, would you honour us in being the first to demonstrate what you believe is strength?"

With his pent up fury Warthog set off tearing towards a dense thicket that would stop most animals in their tracks. Using his finely chiselled tusks, he scattered the tangled vegetation making a clear pathway for Cheetah to follow. When Warthog returned his anger was spent. Cheetah nodded her head in admiration at the speed and efficiency of Warthog's work and all of the animals cried out, "Strength! Strength! We see strength!"

Crocodile smiled and showed an array of razor sharp teeth. "These set of chompers are strength in themselves; however, let me show you how quick and agile I am in the fastest current." Crocodile launched himself into the turbulent waters twisting and turning, diving and resurfacing with grace and undoubted power.

The animals all knew that this stretch of river was dangerous, murky and deep, yet Crocodile dove and brought mud up from the bottom of the riverbed with such ease and grace. The animals all cheered crying, "Strength! Strength! We see strength!"

Cheetah then led the animals through some long tall grass and pointed out a gnarly baobab tree a long way in the distance. "I will race to the tree, round it and be back in circle before you can count the number of teeth in Crocodile's mouth and the feet of this assembly."

"That's impossible!" chided Man.

"What, counting my teeth?" snapped Crocodile.

"No, running that fast. I bet it will take twice as long as Cheetah's boast."

"This is no boast, Man. I will be as good as my word. Just you wait and see!"

Kicking up a cloud of dust, Cheetah sprinted into the distance while Man quickly tottered up the number of feet between them and Baboon hurriedly went to work counting Crocodile's teeth. They were so immersed in their sums that they missed Cheetah's return. She lay lazily looking up at them with a satisfied smile on her lips and asked,

"Have you finished the count?" The smooth, rich velvety tone that purred easily and effortlessly from Cheetah had all of the assembly except for Man muttering appreciation, for she was not even out of breath.

"Hush!" snapped Man impatiently. "I am nearly there. I'll have the tally in a jiffy. Then we can wipe the smile off Cheetah's fa.....ce..."

His words ground to a halt as reality dawned that it was Cheetah who had posed the question.

"Wow, you're quick," stammered Man incredulously and then he joined in gusto as all the animals cheered, "Strength! Strength! We see strength!"

Baboon suddenly sprang up stuttering, "Ccccome on... follow me."

When the animals were once again inside a dense thicket, Baboon leapt towards the tallest tree and scampered up to the top. Holding onto one of the upper branches he suddenly launched himself towards another tree until he had branches of both trees within his grasp. With a whoop and a holler, Baboon tied a knot in the branches creating a bridge between the two trees which he acrobatically swung from.

All of the animals on the ground were applauding and in unison they shouted, "Strength! Strength! We see strength!"

Elephant now plodded slowly toward a large fallen tree that lay strewn across the forest floor. She wrapped her trunk around it and effortlessly lifted it high in the air and carried it towards the river where she gently lowered it so that it reached from bank to bank making a bridge for Cheetah, Man, Warthog, and Baboon to cross over. It is fair to say that the animals would have cried, "Strength! Strength! We see strength!" at the mere sight of Elephant. However, as Crocodile swam in the water and the other animals danced across the newly formed bridge, their cries of, "Strength! Strength! We see strength!" were even heard above Elephant's trumpeting celebrations.

The animals were in high spirits indeed as they turned to see Man standing proudly before them.

"What strength we have seen today. Now be prepared to be amazed, dazzled, and delighted for as they say, always leave the best until last! Sit back and be awed by mighty Man as I gift you and show — the true meaning of strength."

There was generous applause from the excitable Baboon, a roll of the eyes from Warthog, and Cheetah's involuntary expression, "And he claimed I was boasting."

Man sauntered over to a group of trees, oblivious to the reaction of his audience and leapt towards a low hanging branch. He hung there for a few seconds and tried desperately to heave himself up. Grunts and screams followed and then with a mighty effort his body gyrated as he hooked his leg up and over the limb. The exertion proved too much and his grip gave way leaving Man tumbling to the earth below.

A huge round of applause and exclamations of joy emanated from the watching council members.

"Strength!" roared Man.

"No, it wasn't really strength Man… I thought it was funny… I loved how you saved your fall with a forward roll as you landed… It made me smile… I like how you made it look like you lost your grip when you fell… It is because he did lose his grip when he fell!" were several of the comments that spilled from the mouths of his audience.

"Then watch this," growled a disgruntled Man as he climbed onto the fallen tree that spanned the river. He dove into the river and there was an almighty slapping sound as he entered the waters with a resounding belly flop. It winded Man and he flapped around in the waters trying desperately to catch his breath.

His head disappeared under the water and it became obvious to the watching council that Man was in trouble. When he disappeared from sight and failed to surface, Crocodile dove in and pulled Man out. He then had a coughing fit, spluttering and wheezing from being caught in the swirling current of the river.

Man sank to his knees and took his time standing before his peers. When he did his throat was raw and sore and his voice sounded strained as he cried, *"Strength! Strength! That was strength!"*

There was a hushed silence as the group looked on with great concern until finally Elephant spoke, "That wasn't strength, Man. To be perfectly frank with you, I thought it was a little scary."

There were grunts of agreement from the startled council members.

"Get your breath back Man. Take your time," Elephant suggested gently.

"I'm fine!" spat Man with his eyes flashing wildly. He ran his fingers through his long flowing hair and started to flex his muscles. He launched into several poses that had him looking constipated, his friends biting their tongues and straining their faces trying with all their might not to burst out into laughter. They watched as his face turned bright red and they all sensed a combination of fatigue, embarrassment, and above all anger. A single snicker might just set him to burst.

All eyes upon him, Man bent down to lift a large rock into the air. He gritted his teeth, his already red face deepening colour until blotches of purple appeared on his skin and the veins in his neck jutted out like river tributaries. Yet still the rock lay firmly planted on the forest floor.

Man sat on the rock and placed his head in his hands breathing hard from his exertions.

"Cccome on Man, you've got this!" spluttered Baboon.

"Yeah you can do it!" grunted Warthog.

"We believe in you, Man!" echoed the deep calm voice of Elephant.

Man reached down and picked up three small rocks. He stared at them in is hands as the silence stretched between them all. And then he leapt to his feet and tossed the rocks high into the air. He attempted to juggle them and in his mind he saw an array of different patterns being created; however, the reality was very different. As the rocks came crashing toward him, he lost total control. One struck him hard on the head, another landed heavily on his foot, and the third bounced off his knee. Man crumpled onto the earth gyrating around in agony while everyone looked on with concern.

"There," whimpered Man. "Strength," he squeaked, desperately trying to regain some composure by standing up and taking a bow.

"I th th think with practice you'll bbbb be good at it," blurted Baboon.

"Man, I'll give you this, you have a talent for making me laugh," sputtered Warthog, who could suppress his laughter no longer.

"You certainly amazed me," purred Cheetah. "However, I have to say for me, and I think I can speak for the whole assembly here, it simply wasn't strength."

A hush descended upon the gathering as Man looked accusingly into the eyes of all of the council members. One by one they all shook their head in agreement — it was not strength.

Man clenched his jaw and his body tightened as he menacingly whispered, "You want to see strength do you? I'll show you strength. Just you wait here, I'll be back."

He turned on his heels and stormed off grunting and swearing.

The animals looked awkwardly at each other, feeling the blast of Man's fury.

They didn't have long to wait before Man marched into their midst, armed and looking savagely dangerous with a shotgun in his hands. "I've made a firestick, and it can blast things to pieces. This is the ultimate demonstration of strength!" roared Man with a manic gleam in his eye. "Two shots, watch!" he roared as he pulled the trigger and blasted a thick branch clean off the tree.

"You see strength now don't you?" He challenged aiming the barrel at them until it came to rest on the strongest and largest member of the council — Elephant.

The wise pachyderm spoke gently and calmly urging, "Please put that down, Man. We love your antics, we love you. We know you have strength — you just didn't show it falling from the tree, nearly drowning and then dropping rocks on your head, and as for your new firestick, well…"

Elephant was cut off by Man screaming, "The first shot was just a teaser, watch this for strength." Man grinned menacingly into the soulful eyes of Elephant as he gently squeezed the trigger.

A loud crack reverberated through the air. It seemed like everything went in slow motion before speeding up furiously. The horrified council watched as the bulking frame of Elephant crashed to the earth. She lay still before them. For a moment *there was an eerie silence as it slowly registered upon them all that Elephant was dead.*

In the blink of an eye the animals scattered leaving Man standing over the still body of Elephant screaming, "Strength! Strength! I see strength!"

Huddled together in a thicket the fleeing council members put voice to their feelings.

"Wwwwas thththat Stststrength?" mumbled a fearful Baboon.

"No, that wasn't strength," answered Crocodile through a haze of tears.

"No, that was death," whispered Cheetah emphatically.

"Yes, that was death," agreed Warthog pensively.

From that day forward the animals gave Man a wide berth. When he enters the forest now the animals scatter. They watch him from a distance calling to each other to warn them of his movements. They still talk openly to each other, but Man is no longer part of their conversations. When they talk of Man they say, "There goes Man who thinks wilful destruction is proof of strength."

POWER OF THE TALE

Stories are great teachers. Throughout time the greatest prophets have shared wisdom through the power of stories. When I first came across this gem I was struck by the raw power of the tale.

I wonder which pieces spoke most loudly to you?

The separation of human beings from nature is key for me. I recently watched a film on a plane heading from Heathrow to Newark called "Ready Player One," based on a book by Ernest Cline. As movies go I enjoyed the romp; however, the futuristic vision for our species is quite frightening. Set in 2044, a mere twenty odd years ahead of us, the characters spend a huge part of their life living in a virtual world creating avatars to seek adventure through.

For many years now I have written and talked on the subject of how so many human beings have become estranged from nature. People spend more time inside than they do out of doors. Many won't head out in the rain; I have taught so many people the joy of embracing misty rainy days while on pilgrimage in the British Isles and Ireland. As the years keep passing, I see the division between us humans and the natural world growing.

I was talking with a friend about the film and they commented that we are already halfway there, which I concur with. Facebook and other social media sites are rampant with people creating personas to make them look good, a way to present themselves as a type of avatar to a virtual public through a lens of fabrication.

With the rapid explosion in the technological world so many people are addicted to boxes. The cell phone is a shining example of this. My children's generation are the first to have grown up with cell phones being the norm. You only have to watch people eating out, walking beside busy roads, sitting on the bus and train to see heads bowed and eyes fixed to the small screens that are increasingly becoming an extension of the human hand.

Inner cities harbour an intense energy of separation not only from nature but from other human beings. There are so many lonely, angry, and frightened people crammed into the subways. Trees are being ripped up in the name of progress.

Ancient habitats making way for the sprawling masses of an ever increasing human population.

CONVERSATIONS IN THE NATURAL WORLD

When 'Man' shoots 'Elephant' the animals disappear and the speech and understanding is lost between them. Yet anyone who is in tune with nature, who spends significant time connecting to the wildness of the woods, the marshes, the moors, the mountains, the highways, bi-ways, and waterways that are part of the natural world know differently. Nature has an ever present song. If and when we are still and present with our surroundings it is amazing how our creative senses open to the voices of other beings.

In my book, "Magical Crows, Ravens and the Celebration of Death," I write about many incredible conversations I have had with the Corvine family over the years. It may seem strange to someone who has tethered themselves inside the boxes of the world to have animals, trees, the wind, the rocks, and other parts of nature speak to them. For me and many like me it is part and parcel of the symbiotic relationship that is available to all beings who open their hearts to the inherent magic in connecting with all life.

I was talking recently with a two-year group of students studying 'Celtic' shamanic practice with me. I was sharing how important it is to honour any siblings and children that we have in Spirit. I was sharing that in some indigenous cultures the word for soul, breath, and name are from the same root. Some cultures believe that without a name we do not exist.

We were sitting out under the open sky beside 'Bear Pond' in New Jersey, surrounded by the song of the heron, oak, and maple trees and connecting with the story of Llew and Blodeuwedd from the Welsh myths recorded in the Mabinogion.

I shared how important it is to light candles for our siblings and children in Spirit, and how celebrating their birthdays with a cake or a favourite treat is a wonderful way to acknowledge and honour them. There are mothers in the world who have had a miscarriage without even knowing it. There are mothers who have felt a gamut of emotions including sorrow, shame, and anger by which they have never named their children and are not ready to face naming them.

So lighting candles for the mystery children that may have been miscarried in the world is a powerful thing to do. Finding names for those we know to be in Spirit is possible through shamanic work if the mother herself is not ready to name her children.

My mother has a daughter and a son in Spirit. Her daughter, my sister, reached out to me and named herself; as a shamanic practitioner I was able to journey to find a name for my brother. It is a joy and a privilege to celebrate them each year. I thank my partner Joyce for deepening this relationship with my siblings as she has practiced this with her own family in spirit for many, many years.

I share this story here as when my sister came she showed herself in the form of an elephant. I was in Northumberland in the North East of England questing out on the land. I had spent the night alone out on a bluff where the ancestors carved four animal figures on a wall. It is a powerful place and one that I discovered magically when I was out looking for a stone circle. The farmer whose land these etchings are on told me that there was no stone circle; however, he divulged that there was a place of ancestral interest known as Goats Crag. He told me that some people believe that the four carvings there are of goats. With a twinkle in his eye, he shared that he believed they are actually horses.

When I first saw them I saw horses too. I knew on that day I would quest there as my last name is Steed. I have one brother who lives in Torquay and then my two siblings in spirit. There are four of us Steeds — it was as if the horses on the rock were calling me home.

In the morning sunrise of my quest, my sister showed herself to me. I had stayed awake through a chilly night on the crag and in the morning glory I saw and heard her in the sky. She was in the form of a cloud in the shape of an elephant. She laughed out loud and the rippling sound became her name. It was Nell-E. I heard her quite distinctly asking me, "Do you get it? Nell-E?" I burst out laughing because I did get it. I have spoken backwards as all my life, particularly so as a child when I would joke with my living brother that he was nhoJ treboR deetS and I was werdnA deetS. Here was Nell-E the elephant — Ellen Steed. Tears of joy streamed down my face as she celebrated with me.

She then guided me to a tree stump down by a waterfall which has two unique sides to it. One looks just like a horse, the other side is distinctly an elephant!

As I sat sharing with the two-year group about honouring our siblings and children a dragonfly flew directly in front of my face. It hovered there as I spoke and I laughed saying, "Look it is

Nell-E, she is with us!" The dragonfly continued to hover before me. As I continued talking using my hands as I do, the dragonfly landed on one of my outstretched fingers. I held my hand steady and continued sharing the importance of names and connecting with our kin and the dragonfly stayed for heartbeat after heartbeat. Nell-E perched there for some time before flying off.

The point I am making here is that not only does nature talk to us, the ancestors are talking too — if we only have the heart to listen!

OTHER GEMS

Other pieces that resonate from the story and stir poignant questions inside of me relate to how Man gets bent out of shape when he feels laughed at. It is never fun to have people laugh at us rather than with us. Sometimes we laugh out of embarrassment, sometimes it is in persecution, sometimes it is involuntary. It is amazing how slapstick comedy tickles our fancy; Man had quite the comedian's routine down and if he had played it to the full perhaps a genuine gift of bringing laughter to the gathering would have been seen as strength. As it was, he was fuelled by anger and sought retribution on those that he perceived had wronged him.

A saying that I often use is, "when we get bent out of shape it is down to us as it is our shape to bend." It can be challenging not to take it personally in the world. We all desperately try to fit in when in reality the only place it is important to fit in is our own heart.

One last piece that struck me from the tale that I am keen to share is the late arrival of Man. I know when working with spirit there is no such thing as linear time. Yet in this world of group agreements, when a community, workplace etc. have designated a time to begin it is so important to honour that agreement in my book. Man being late and swanning in without an apology is rude to say the least. One thing to think on is that if we are ten minutes late and a group have to wait for us, we are more than ten minutes late. For depending on how many people have gathered you can multiply that ten minutes by the number of people in attendance i.e. ten people equals one hundred minutes — an hour and forty minutes late!

WAKING UP

The power of the alienation of 'Man' through the death of 'Elephant' reverberated through me when I first read this story. What I know to be true is that the Universe is always speaking to us. Most of us, however, are too busy to listen.

As I have alluded to, with all of our technological advances, so many people alienate themselves from the natural world. Many are scared of nature and if they do step into the woods it is often with their phone set to camera mode to snap whatever they see. It is amazing how some choose to have music blaring from their iPod to keep them or their children entertained rather than connect to the song and poetry of nature's artistic canvas. Some enter with a view to destroy or conquer. The land is sold off to the highest bidder, the life force squeezed out of it, cut down, manipulated, manicured, poisoned, and despoiled for profit, vanity, and an ego that boasts of our dominion over all other life forms.

I believe in the interconnected nature of all beings. This concept is one that has grown roots and wings within my heart over many years as I have developed a love affair with the land. It is one that is now being embraced by more and more seekers who are looking to live outside of the lines of conventional thought. It is one that the scientific world has also acknowledged and it is a joy to see that magic and science are finding compatibility in each other's arms. What a joy it is to witness science and spirituality converging on a bridge of understanding.

Ancient mystics and wise sages throughout the ages have shared the 'Universal Truth' that we are all one. Science, along with us human beings, is having an awakening in the acceptance and understanding of the wisdom within this truth.

However, as the light-bulbs go on and we begin to plug in to this idea of oneness, there are still many who stumble around in the dark and others who look to sever the connection out of fear and greed.

My life experience has opened me up to the power of the wild nature that resides within us and around us. I have entered the forest without the gun and the animal, vegetable, and mineral kingdom have spoken to me in a multitude of ways.

In July 2107, the elephants reached out to me and asked me to share a story with my human sisters and brothers. This is a tale of heart, wisdom, and what I and the elephants that I spoke with believe is — *the true meaning of strength*.

Before I reveal the majesty of their teachings, I would first like to explore my journey to stand in their presence, a journey that was a prequel to an amazing encounter that I will share anon. I will also explore the elephant in the role of an iconic symbol of India and reveal the reality of what goes on behind the mask. I will also expand upon the worldwide treatment of elephants and share some myths and fables that honour these wise pachyderms.

INDIA

I visited Varkala in Kerala, India in 2013. I was wandering the land after a twenty-six-year hiatus to see how both India and I had changed. It was a glorious opportunity to witness the changes within the land and my own three bodies — mentally, physically, and spiritually.

I had first stepped into this colourful country of contrast in 1987. It was a profound journey that shaped me. When we step outside of our comfort zones we offer ourselves an opportunity for transformation. In 1987, there were no cell phones or internet and in the south of India there were very few tourists. I strolled on my own and I embarked on a life changing pathway for three-and-a-half months which felt more like three-and-a-half years. I met myself and entered into a profound relationship with both my own inner landscape and with Hindustan — the great goddess — Mother India.

A skinny boy from Bury St. Edmunds who grew up with a belief in faeries, dragons, and a magical world of stories left the shores of his homeland and found himself in the greatest story of his life — one of his own making — his own living story. A boy left his home shores to return a man.

Many of us struggle to fit in to this fast paced world. As a youngster I was incredibly thin; I felt gawky and was teased incessantly by much bigger peers. It was weird being in the physical body of a little boy as my friends matured into men. I left school at sixteen, I was eighteen before my pubic hair grew in, and in my twenties before I started shaving.

I coined a phrase later in life to express this feeling of isolation — 'sacred outcast.' A term that I own with genuine affection as I learnt to fall in love with my own self, not from a place of ego, rather from a place of heart. In so doing I no longer felt the rejections of my past as I accepted myself for the beautiful soul that I truly am.

India opened me up in 1987 and continued to bring riches to my heart-fire, the hearth of my physical body in both 2013 and again when I returned for a third time in 2017.

VARKALA 2013

I have written in depth about my experience with the crows in my book, *Magical Crows, Ravens and the Celebration of Death.* For those who have gleaned the gems from that tale you will know that I had never intended to go to Varkala. In fact, I was unaware of its existence in 2013. Spirit drew me into its folds and magic happened. The connection with the crows and the ancestors will be carried with me always; however, I was blessed to hear another voice. A voice that was the driving force for the creation of this book.

I left the sanctuary of the retreat centre where I was staying and wandered towards the sweltering hustle and bustle of town. I waved down a tuk-tuk and hopped aboard the small motorised rickshaw as I went in search of a different kind of sanctuary, a dwelling place for several elephants that had been recommended to me to visit.

My thoughts drifted to how elephants are revered in India. They are one of the icons for the tourist industry. Statues, t-shirts, and an assortment of paraphernalia are adorned with the

symbol of the elephant and of course the elephant god
Ganesha.

GANESHA

The goddess Parvati, consort to Lord Shiva, enjoyed the ritual of bathing alone and undisturbed. Their residence on Mount Kailash was perched high in the mountainous region of the Himalayas. She had set the task of guarding her door to Nandi. Now Nandi was faithful to the task; however, his allegiance was to Shiva. So when Shiva came home and asked his loyal Bull to step aside, Nandi did so willingly.

Parvati bristled when Shiva walked upon her nakedness brazenly without an invite. She pondered on the matter, acknowledging that part of her frustration stemmed from the fact that Shiva had such a devoted guardian of the gateways. She craved a loyal guardian, someone who would stand for her and block the pathway to the inner sanctum of their home.

So, she found a solution. She created life: a loving steadfast son. Some say she gathered clay, mud, and bark and other precious elements from the earth. Some will tell you that she simply breathed life into turmeric paste collected from her body during a bathing ritual. Others will swear it was sandalwood that she peeled from her body and afterwards, by sprinkling waters from the Ganges, a beautiful baby boy was born. Whether it was a combination of these, or other properties were used in the creation of life, the resulting birth was a strong young son. Finally, Parvati had someone who was true to her, an unbreakable bond between mother and son.

With such a loving guardian blocking entry into the sanctuary of her bath house, Parvati breathed easily as she stepped into a ritual cleanse.

It was at this time that Lord Shiva returned home to find a stranger blocking his path. If he thought his mere presence would grant him access he was to be sorely disappointed. His commanding voice fell on deaf ears. Some will tell you he received a blow to his head from the staff the boy wielded. Others tell of Lord Shiva commanding his army to remove the obstacle in his path. If it was indeed Shiva's army that set upon the boy they were rebuffed and defeated for one thing that is agreed upon by all who know this tale is it took Shiva himself to face this unknown force.

Shiva's anger reached to boiling point and in his rage he struck off the head of the courageous boy. Still seething with anger, he turned on his heels and strode away from the corpse of this stranger, oblivious to the fact he had struck down and killed his own son.

When Parvati emerged she was distraught. A tempest of grief and anger emanated from her being. It threatened to engulf the townsfolk and spread beyond with the destruction of creation itself. She vowed vengeance upon all beings until the murderer of her son stepped forward.

Lord Brahma, the Creator, took issue with this and confronted Shiva. He urged Shiva to have the courage to face Parvati and take responsibility for his actions.

Some will tell you that Shiva's confession prompted Parvati to make two conditions of her own. Their son Ganesha was to be brought back to life and he was to be worshipped before all of the other gods. Many will share that Brahma played a significant role in breathing life into the boy. Some say it was Shiva's men who retrieved the head of an elephant, others remark it was Shiva himself who took the head from the first animal that he met along his path and some say it was Brahma who looked for the first animal that was lying down with their head to the north. All agree that it was a wise, strong elephant head that Shiva placed onto the body of Ganesha and that he declared to all that the rebirthed boy was his son.

Ganesha was given the status of being foremost amongst the gods. He is known as the remover of obstacles and carvings of his likeness are to be found at the entrance to many temples throughout India.

POWER OF THE TALE

This ancient tale holds morsels of wisdom within its folds. I wonder how many of us have difficulty in voicing our truth. Parvati yearns on having privacy in the sanctuary of her bath house, yet instead of confronting Shiva directly she first sets Shiva's own gatekeeper Nandi to be her guard and then pits son against father when Nandi so willingly steps aside.

It takes courage in this world to communicate our needs clearly and effectively without attacking a person for their behaviour. So many people will skim around the problem creating more problems through first venting and then gossiping about another's actions rather than going directly to the person they are challenged by. Instead, they create war in the worlds through the poison of their thoughts and words as they lash out with their tongue behind the person's back.

This verbal tirade that creates tangles in the loom of our own lives. It takes the hero to face their fears, to bring gentle strength to their words, and communicate with the person that they are challenged with directly.

Each of us will know fear as we face the adventure of life. The hero knows the taste of fear as well as anyone. What defines the greatness within the hero is a capacity to love, for a hero always loves more than they fear.

I love this nugget of wisdom. Let's allow this to sink more deeply into our bones as I repeat it here — *a hero always loves more than they fear*!

Each of us has the choice in any given situation to be the hero of our life story or to be stuck in the role of victim. What if more of us awoke to our own inner hero and stepped into the shadow of fear with love to guide our way?

BLOCKING THE PATH

It is interesting to note that in offering his life in the service as a gatekeeper, essentially blocking the pathway to all and sundry, Ganesha becomes known as a deity who removes all obstacles.

Each of us will face obstacles that block our way. Taking a sword and hacking down another to get where we want to go can create great chaos in the world. I wonder how many of us give someone that good tongue lashing (I see the tongue as the sword of our heads) and let our anger drive the way in a spinning out act of war rage. How many of us create devastation that cuts down our loved ones, our family and extended family members, in our workplaces, and community. Careless words that strip someone of their dignity or force them into a defensive stance whereby they then launch an attack on us and the two of us slash away at each other in a vicious assault that can cause deep festering wounds.

I wonder how many parents bully and intimidate their children to force home their point stopping at nothing to win an argument.

STANDING IN OUR POWER

Ganesha has a job assigned to him to protect his mother's doorway. He dies in service to an oath, an agreement to carry out his mother's request. We are incredibly vulnerable when we stand naked in front of others. When we close a doorway and lock it as Parvati thinks she has with Nandi, it is a violation to have someone come crashing into the protective sanctuary to stare at our nakedness. Ganesha takes on an honourable role and is willing to die to protect his mother and honour his oath as her protector.

It takes immense courage to stand in the fullness of our power and to honour the oaths we make in our lives. It takes strength of character to be willing to die to protect the rights of others. I wonder though where we are like Ganesha and Shiva, whereby we fail to communicate with each other and choose to lash out as possibly Ganesha does in some versions of the story (he wields a staff at Shiva), which is like poking a stick at a hornet's nest.

OVERCOMING OBSTACLES

Ganesha's gift is helping others to overcome obstacles and the story certainly lends itself to the exploration of where do each of us face hardships and overcome them. How the knocks of life prepare us to look at our rough edges so we can polish and smooth these edges for the highest good of our life's purpose.

PURIFICATION RITUALS

It is interesting that Parvati looks to purify her body in what may on the surface seem like a physical purification. In the act of this ritual her mental body and spiritual body spin out to the point where she is ready to cast a raging tempest that will destroy all of creation.

I wonder how well each of us looks after all three of our bodies. Purification rituals to honour and build muscle in the physical, mental, and spiritual journey of our lives is a paramount piece for personal growth in my world. I invite each of us to take an inventory of how we honour these bodies of ours and what kind of commitments we are willing to make to expand and strengthen them.

SACRED STORIES

I know there is more to this story for a hungry and thirsty soul who is willing to delve into the spaces between the spaces and glean new perspectives. To use the eye of Imbas, the all seeing eye, to discover another pathway to ourselves through exploring the threads within this ancient tale.

When we peek within the folds of a story we cannot get it wrong. For stories speak to us all in different ways. I have offered a glimpse into some of the strands that spoke to me in the loom of my life. In sitting with these questions the tapestry becomes brighter, my life journey clearer because I have sat with these questions. In discovering different facets of myself I have activated new life force by being the power of the medicine that I have personally gleaned here. I hope you are called to embark on your journey of self-discovery and transformation through the stories and insights here. If so enjoy the ride!

ORAL TRADITIONS

Any story written down to our early ancestors made no sense —
for once written the tale becomes a fixed record of events, yet
stories were told orally for they were continually shifting to
meet the unfolding needs of a participating audience.

I have spoken on this before, for as an author I know that in
creating a new work there comes a time when I have to let go
and send it out into the world, to speak its voice in that
moment. For a week, a month, and certainly in a year and a
day's time, I would find things to tweak, to shift, and change as I
have shifted and changed. It is why some writers fall short of
completing a work. So many of us in life seek perfection when
the perfection is in the imperfection! Living in the moment of
what something is today and celebrating it fully is an authentic
and treasured gift!

A SANCTUARY BY NAME

I was about to walk into one of the shadow sides of this exotic
land as I headed to the elephant sanctuary in Kerala. One that
would tear at my heartstrings and startle my senses. There is a
well of suffering that oozes blood, grime, and tears on this
planet. The elephant sanctuary that I arrived at is part of the
darkness that feeds human dominion over other life forms in
this world.

The driver pulled up outside the imposing gates to the sanctuary. I disembarked and pushed the gateway open and I stepped inside. All of the elephants were chained up. Several stern looking men sat along a wall staring at me. The rickshaw driver appeared and in his broken English explained that they were the workers who looked after the elephants. Unfortunately, their English was poor and although we had difficulty communicating verbally, their body language and energy made me feel unwelcome.

I paid the requested rupees for the entrance fee and then I walked slowly towards the nearest elephant. If you have never been close to an elephant before it is not only their size that impacts you, it is their majesty. When I looked into the eyes of this repressed chained up being I saw an ancientness which reflected a deep pool of wisdom. My heart went out to him. I had understood the sharp command to stay back and so I knew I was not able to physically embrace him so I connected with him from my heart through Amrun.

AMRUN – THE SONG THAT SINGS US

All indigenous tribes have a song that sings us. A song that comes from Spirit and can be woven to connect the threads of this interconnected universe. In the Celtic tradition this is called Amrun. I have talked about it both in *Magical Crows…* and in another book, *13 Steps to Bringing Magic into Your Life*. For now, I will share that it comes through us when we get out of the head and into the heart.

I open my mouth and become an instrument for Spirit to sing through me. On this day I brought the song of hope, love, and gentle strength to all of the elephants that I was allowed to approach. I first shared my disappointment and the sadness that I felt in my fellow human beings who seek dominion over the land and all beings. I let them know that it was not in my power to break their chains; however, I could bring them a gift of song. I asked their permission before I sang to them and waited to sense their answer before I became a hollow bone and with an overwhelming "Yes!" ringing in my bones, I became the song that sings me.

I felt humbleness and a deep gratitude to the openness that I felt between us as I stood before each of these magnificent captives.

Yet I left the sanctuary conflicted. I am not so naïve to think animal abuse is not rampant in the world. I was, however, disturbed to see an iconic animal of a country that I had thought to be a sacred part of the landscape so ill-treated.

I had done my best to offer something to the elephants and yet it seemed so little. When I returned to the retreat centre I mulled over the stark difference of a word that I readily applied to where I was staying – *sanctuary*! The abundant flowers in the garden, the clean spacious rooms, the friendly nature of the staff, and the atmosphere of this peaceful haven that I had chosen to stay in offered true sanctuary.

My understanding of this word is that it means a refuge, a safe oasis, a space that offers protection and security.

The elephant sanctuary was a far cry from this definition. I later looked up the Hindi meaning of this word. The translation into English offers these three choices:

1. An area around an altar.
2. A shelter from danger or hardship.
3. A consecrated place where sacred objects are kept.

None of these rang true to my experience with the elephants. Perhaps the elephants are viewed as sacred objects so number three comes into play. Yet from my perspective using the word 'object' diminishes the true nature of the sacredness of a living being.

DOMINION OVER LIFE

I was snapped out of my thoughts by the smiling figure of Feroz who had asked me about my day. Feroz was the heartbeat of the retreat centre. Each day his presence brought a light that enriched all who crossed his path. I shared my dismay at the harsh nature and poor treatment that I had witnessed at the elephant sanctuary. He was genuinely shocked and wondered whether I had visited a different place than the one that was in their guide book of recommended places to see.

As I described the conditions he felt sure that I had been taken to a completely different centre.

The elephant is considered by many Hindus to be the embodiment of Lord Ganesha. In light of this you would think elephants would command high status within India's cultural framework. Perhaps from the outside it looks as if they do. The pomp and ceremony, the bright colours and music all lends itself to the appearance of celebration — with elephants at the heart of it. However, when you dig more deeply into how elephants are treated a very different picture is to be found, where smoke and mirrors and harsh cruel treatment offers only degradation, pain, and a long drawn out death to these wise pachyderms.

There is so much abuse in this world. The human condition of feeling more important that the land and the beings we share this miraculous earth with runs rampant. Unless the abuse directly affects us or is in our face, we appear oblivious to it, or we choose to skip over the surface of it rather than facing the impact of the devastation to the parties involved. So many of us are ignorant to the pain and suffering of our fellow participants in this earthly experience. Others are wilfully blind, turning away from the atrocities unwilling to acknowledge and take any responsibility for them. As for tourists who venture into countries like India, so many of them are oblivious to the brutal conditions that are part and parcel of the shadow side of an elephant's journey. The harsh reality is that they are stolen from the wild and beaten into submission to accept a rider so the goggle-eyed tourists can marvel at sitting astride an elephant's back.

I see this attitude of dominion over other life forms as a disease that has become an accepted part of our interaction with the natural world. Albeit the appalling conditions of farmed chickens to the vast array of animals used for experimentation – testing for treatments to help cure human diseases, breeding, defence research, and toxicology with the universities, medical schools, defence establishments, pharmaceutical and cosmetic companies all playing their part in this subjugation of other beings.

The practice of stealing elephants from their natural habitats and then training them and taming them has gone on for over four thousand years with the first records surfacing from the time of the Indus Valley civilization around 2,000 BCE.

In the same year that I walked into the elephant sanctuary Sangita Iyer, an Indian journalist living in Toronto returned to her roots and visited Kerala. She, like I, was horrified how the elephants, supposedly sacred animals, were living torturous lives. She has been the driving force behind a must see documentary, *Gods in Shackles.* The barbaric treatment of these gigantic beings brought her to tears.

She goes on to share how male elephants are starved and beaten occasionally to death during and after their musth cycle, the mating season. Male elephant bulls walk for miles in the wild seeking mates, fighting other bulls along the way. In captivity they are deprived of their freedom spending years of captivity in chains. They have no mate, so to subdue them the handlers starve them of food and water.

She shares how elephants have been intentionally blinded by their handlers, how some are deliberately maimed. The atrocities go on and on. And for what?

Pomp and ceremony for religious gatherings, parades, processions, tourism, wedding rituals, shop and hotel openings, logging activities, political party campaigns, trade fairs, and ultimately the bottom line — financial gain.

According to a BBC news report in April 2018, there are over 4,000 captive elephants in India with the World Wild Life Fund reporting that there could be as few as 20,000 in the wild. According to the International Union for Conservation of Nature, the wild Indian elephant population has declined by around 50% in the last 75 years. Media reports also suggest that more than 70 captive elephants have died because of abuse and neglect in just three states – Kerala, Rajasthan, and Tamil Nadu — between 2015 and 2017.

Not only are young elephants snatched from the wild by poachers, the mothers and other herd members who look to protect their young are often slaughtered in the process.

A captured elephant calf is then subjected to a practice known as 'pajan.' Locked in a pen, tethered in ropes to prevent them from moving, isolated from their kin, they are then tortured to break their spirits. This brutal practice includes beating them with rods, chains, and bullhooks. The bullhook is a rod with a sharp metal hook that is used to strike the elephant; knives and nails are also used to stab the subject into submission.

The list of cruelty goes on. Elephants transported in open-back trucks have been known to fall out causing serious injuries and death. So many of them suffer problems with their feet from standing on concrete platforms in captivity, pounding the streets on hot road surfaces and standing for days in their own waste. Then there are the tears and abrasions from the sharp hooks on the chains that break the skin causing deep wounds and infections which quite commonly go untreated.

They also encounter problems from heat exhaustion without access to water sources or a dirt bath to cool them as they would in the wild.
Elephants in captivity suffer from eye disorders. Their eyes are as delicate and sensitive as human beings. Long exposure to the glaring sun during their roles in festivals and the practice of some handlers who blow powdered glass into their eyes to remove so-called films, leaves many elephants with permanently impaired vision and even total loss of sight.

The bull's tusks are blunted by removing the sharp tips with chainsaws which is not only a violation, it has to be incredibly stressful.

It is a lucrative business renting out elephants who are so often neglected by their captors. It is extortionate amounts of money too, with a prize bull elephant earning up to 70,000 rupees a day for an appearance at a religious festival in the height of the season. That is equivalent to over $1,000/£750. Less money spent on the elephant's welfare means more profit in the coffers! Kerala has 10,000 festivals during December to May each year. Elephants are painted in bright colours with rich heavy garments adorning their bodies. They are also required to carry up to 800kg/1,763lbs on their backs comprising of a deity, its frame, and four men. All of this while having up to four legs shackled, both walking through the streets amid noisy revellers dancing to loud music while letting off firecrackers and being required to stand in one place for extended periods of time.

There is also the increased population of humans and our desire to claim wild land as our own to consider on the effect of the elephant population. As humans encroach on the rapidly shrinking forest habitats on the planet, wild life all around the globe are being forcibly evicted from their natural homes. Elephants have traditional migratory routes known as corridors.

With farmland replacing forest land and roads and rail lines springing up, elephants are in danger of being killed in collisions and to being attacked by farmers whose crops they trample down. There is also the danger from electrocution from the unprotected power lines that have been installed along these corridors.

There are temples who according to the Animal Welfare Board of India are violating numerous animal welfare laws. Add to this — many elephants in Rajasthan and Kerala are illegal in the fact that they do not have any legal documentation regarding ownership.

The depravation and sordid world that is part of a captive elephant's day to day experience is starting to come to light thanks to people like Sangita Iyer who urges people to boycott India's temple festivals that incorporate the use of elephants and refrain from visiting temples where elephants are kept captive. It is also important for tourists to refuse to take part in riding on their backs.

There is some movement in that the documentary, *Gods in Shackles*, is garnering Worldwide attention. It also has been screened by the government in Kerala at its legislative assembly.

There are now discussions taking place within India's government regarding the role of elephants in cultural festivals. There is genuine hope that bans could be imposed to reduce and possibly stop the exploitation of these noble beings.

The phrase 'wake up' comes to mind for we live in a fragile time for many beings on the planet. Elephants have been part of the story of planet earth for eons. Fossil records indicate that more than 300 species of elephant have graced the earth over a period of 55 million years. The human evolution began around six million years ago with homo-sapiens evolving only recently — about 200,000 years ago. Interestingly, the term homo-sapiens means wise man in Latin. Perhaps it's time for the wisdom to kick in! For without it we are in serious danger of being the generation that lets elephants become extinct.

The mistreatment of elephants is a worldwide phenomenon and I wonder how many of us are aware of how close we are to seeing the extinction of this wise being from the wild places of our world today. On the flipside there is hope — I believe that this book along with the voices of others who are advocating for better welfare of all of our sisters and brothers in all of the kingdoms, animal, vegetable, and mineral may yet lead to an evolution of the human race.

INTELLIGENCE TO MATCH THE BRAIN SIZE

All beings are powerful and all have a variety of gifts to bring to the world! In researching this book, I have gained a whole new perspective on the true meaning of strength, wisdom, and sheer wonder that these intelligent giants bring to the globe. It became self-evident to me why Spirit would lead Shiva to choosing an elephant's head for his son.

Elephants never forget. Some researchers claim that this saying is of Greek origin replacing an earlier saying — *Camels never forget.* Yet I grew up with the elephant version and I am sure many of you reading this did too.

The truth is that elephants, like us humans, sometimes do forget — yet there is overwhelming scientific evidence that upholds some truth within this old saying. For elephants have a great capacity to remember and retain. Elephants are remarkably intelligent beings.

Their brains are similar to a human's brain in both structure and complexity. They boast the largest brain of any land mammal weighing in at around eleven pounds/five kilograms. However, size does not equate to intelligence. What does is the ratio between actual brain mass and predicted brain mass — an elephant has an impressive encephalization quotient. They have as many neurons and synapses as a human and their hippocampus and cerebral cortex is highly developed.

So what does this all mean? Quite simply, an elephant has a complex and multi-skilled capacity to remember and retain information beyond rote memorization as well as the ability to problem solve.

It also means that they are one of the few animals alongside humans to experience post-traumatic stress disorder. This is a major factor to consider as we delve into the way elephants are treated in our world both within sanctuaries and the wild.

They mostly live in herds led by a matriarchal elder. These herds usually have deep family bonds. The herd is comprised of females and young males who have yet come to sexual maturity. I have personally witnessed herds with as little as two members and some that have been twenty-five strong. It is reported that elephants know every member within the herd, recognising as many as thirty of their tribe by sight and/or smell.

ROOTED IN SCIENTIFIC DISCOVERY

In 2007, scientists from the University of St. Andrews in the Kingdom of Fife conducted an experiment in the Amboseli National Park in Kenya. They placed urine samples in front of a cow herd; interestingly, they discovered that elephants "acted up" when they smelled urine from elephants outside of their own herd.

The herd is incredibly protective of each other. Sisters of a pregnant mother provide support both during the birthing process and for the baby's formative years. The calf has to learn how to search for food and water, to take on specific roles within the herd, and the males are taught how to look for a mate.

MORE INTERESTING FACTS

When the herd is confronted by elephants that they do not recognise they instinctively bunch together to protect their young.

The elders within the tribe have developed memories through their years of experience, building up a strong social knowledge. Elephants who survived a drought in their youth can recognise warning signs that aid survival rates in later years. The phenomenal memories of these older matriarchs enable them to recall routes to watering holes, some of which are hundreds of kilometres apart.

According to Matt Lewis, a Senior Program Officer for the World Wildlife Fund's Species Conservation Program, research has shown that these matriarchal elders who have experienced a previous drought will guide the herd to more fertile land whereby younger matriarchs who lack this experience are more likely to stay put.
This ability to remember and distinguish signs of danger plays a significant role in increasing the numbers within the herd. Their ability to recognise friends from foe through smell and/or contact calls enables them to make quicker decisions in helping the herd protect themselves. With the trust that is built up by these strong wise elders, the herd feel more comfortable and more calves are produced and survive.

Once a male is ready to mate, usually around the age of fourteen, the bull leaves the herd sometimes to wander alone, sometimes to wander with other males, and sometimes according to the research of Joyce Poole, head of the Elephant Program of Kenya Wildlife Service in Africa from 1990 – 1994 and a leading pioneer in the study of elephant social behaviour and communication, they attach themselves to other family groups. Some male elephants move from one family group to another spending eighty percent of their time within different herds up until the age of twenty-five.

Males cluster in larger groups when food is scarce and mating opportunities are abundant.

Similar to the effect of a poacher taking a matriarch from the herd, losing an older bull impacts the next generation. There is a lot of interaction and wisdom imparted to younger bulls through the roughhousing and the social influence that the elders display to the younger males.

ZOOS

I have never been a fan of zoos. I remember as a boy peering into the cages of trapped birds in the Abbey Gardens in my home town of Bury St. Edmunds. Perhaps my own free natured spirit felt the weight of the bars, sturdy locks, and hidden keys more heavily than some of my peers.

I have listened to the argument that zoos protect species that would otherwise be endangered out in the wild; that providing them with a space is a way to preserve them. Yet, with the information that we now have available, I wonder if the general populace is aware of how in many situations the captivity of animals is detrimental to their welfare.

As I researched the effect of zoos on elephants I was staggered to find out the adverse effect that they have had on these intelligent beings.

Many experts in the field of elephant study agree that with the new found knowledge regarding the mental intellect of elephants, locking them up is inexcusable.

I came across statistics compiled by a former elephant caretaker, Dan Koehl. He maintains a thorough database of captive elephants around the globe. According to his records there are close to 8,000 elephants in some form of captivity. Over 1,500 of these are in zoos and safari parks, the rest are found in elephant camps where they provide tourists with an opportunity to ride upon their backs, circuses, temples, sanctuaries, and private residencies.

A recent study of close to 300 elephants that reside in North American Zoos, accredited by the Association of Zoos and Aquariums (AZA), was conducted by Koehl and a team of researchers including animal welfare expert Cheryl Meehan. The physical and mental health of the elephants was examined and documented including blood and hormone tests and veterinary reports. The results indicate that about seventy-five percent of the elephants are overweight or obese, that foot and musculoskeletal health problems are common, and three quarters of them have developed behavioural tics, pacing, swaying, rocking, and continual head bobbing.

Is it any wonder that elephants develop sore feet and joint problems? The sheer size of them, weighing up to eight tonnes, becomes a major factor when they are outside of their natural habitat. An elephant in the wild has space to wander and forage. Along with the exercise that is an everyday occurrence for an elephant that roams free in nature, they have an opportunity to rub their feet on the earth, digging into the ground which helps to keep their foot pads moist and therefore supple.

Those in captivity are often exposed to concrete and tarmac surfaces which create sores and cracks to toenails and the fat pads on their feet. Add to this that many captive elephants are standing in urine and faeces for long periods of their day. Imagine if our feet were exposed to rougher harder surfaces that created sores, abrasions, and cuts upon them and then we stood in our own waste for hours on end! One article that I read online from 2006 shares that the Smithsonian National Zoo in Washington, D.C. had to euthanize and elephant because of a foot infection that year. A 2012 expose by the Seattle Times claimed that 390 elephants have died over a fifty-year period in

AZA accredited zoos and most of those were due to injuries or conditions relating to their feet!

Of course, elephants die in the wild. However, I find it challenging to accept that we live in a world where it socially acceptable to cage and imprison wildlife let alone discovering that we have to kill them from time to time because the facilities we have provided for them are inadequate for their welfare.

A lack of exercise and a diet of calorie rich foods that are alien to their natural habitats has a toll on the physical condition of the captive elephant; however, the mental toll is higher. Elephants are social beings who live in herds for years on end; they develop deep and meaningful relationships. In zoos, calves that are born are often separated from their mothers as they are sent to other zoos. Many elephants get separated from other adults during their captivity and are often subject to living in compact enclosures within small groups with little to stimulate them each day.

Some zoos mix males and females in a way that would not happen in their natural environment. Adult males are often confined to their own area and moved on if they get too boisterous and lustful. Current research identifies how misunderstood the male is; the bulls are not the solitary figures that was once thought to be the order of the day, they socialize extensively with their kind.

SOME ARGUE IN FAVOUR OF CAPTIVITY

Dr. Michael Hutchins, former AZA Director who has published many peer reviewed articles about elephant management in accredited zoos argues that facilities such as Disney's Animal Kingdom, Dallas Zoo, San Diego Zoo and Smithsonian' National Zoo, provide ample acres with space for social interaction, feeding, bathing, and wallowing. He believes that as long as proper care can be provided that the environmental enrichment programs provide significant contributions to education, science, and conservation. His belief is the benefits of captivity outweigh the costs.

He admits that there is a trade-off between zoo exhibition and animal welfare. His vision is for more elephants to be imported so that family groups can be housed together in much larger more naturalistic settings. That zoos are able to improve elephant husbandry and reproduction so that the population is sustainable in the long term and that better care is afforded to bulls in captivity. He also believes that relationships between zoos and circuses become a thing of the past. That elephants should not be used as they are in circuses for entertainment value.

I DON'T BUY IT

These arguments for supporting zoos seems tenuous to me. The fact that he says there is a trade-off between exhibition and welfare is a huge red flag in my book! And although there are a number of facilities looking to provide elephants with more space and activities to challenge their intellect, many facilities lack the funds and have no way to re-create an environment that resembles the complex social issues and physical requirements of a thriving herd.

I find it challenging to accept the argument that a zoo provides the viewing public with an education about elephants given that most zoos have created an alien environment for them to live in. Surely nature documentaries following the activities of a herd in the wild are going to provide a more comprehensive education.

Currently the life expectation of elephants in captivity is considerably lower that their brothers and sisters in the wild!

I wonder where you stand on the issue of locking up other beings in the name of their best interest. Do you buy into this argument of animal welfare or do you see it as a guise to satiate our own desires for parcelling up the animal kingdom as we have the land in the name of progress, entertainment, and education?

Are locked cages not prisons? Are chains not a form of slavery and servitude?

Ed Stewart, co-founder of the Performing Animal Welfare Society talking about the 930-hectare sanctuary that provides space for captive elephants, admits that this haven is inadequate for them stating, "Elephants should not be in captivity — period." A wild elephant is generally a healthier elephant than one in captivity. Why? Simply put, the social structure is incorrect, climate is a factor, and the foods that they forage on are too often different.

What I have gleaned in my own research as a layman looking at the confinement of elephants is that they are highly intelligent beings. Captivity limits them. Replicating the wild is an impossible task.

Stephen Harris and colleagues of Bristol University conducted a study of captive elephants in zoos in the late noughties (2000's). He gave a succinct answer when asked whether it is possible to

keep an elephant physically and mentally healthy in a zoo —
"No."

Along with the foot problems, tics, cramped conditions,
abnormal gaits, weight problems, infertility, and mortality rates
he also concluded that many zoo elephants do not get enough
rest as they do not like to lie on the hard stone and other
unnatural surfaces provided for them.

Dr. Joshua Plotnik, founder of Think Elephants International,
believes that although all elephants ought to be in the wild, it is
not realistic. A mass release of captive elephants is not feasible
even if there was enough wild habitat to accommodate them.
He argues for phasing out elephant captivity by sourcing
lucrative jobs for elephant caretakers and maintaining the
existing wild Asian elephant population through conservation
measures.

Dr. Cynthia Moss moved from the USA to Africa in 1968 and has
worked with wildlife ever since. She set up the Amboseli Trust
for Elephants in 2001 and is an expert in the field of elephant
research, networking globally with elephant scientists and
conservation in Africa and Asia. She is in favour of seeing zoos in
the USA and Europe stop breeding and ceasing the importation
of elephants.

Considering elephants are not currently being bred in zoos for the purpose of reintroduction to the wild, the only reasons I can see to continue breeding is:

1. Fear based, whereby we stick our heads in the sand and refuse to take responsible for the global greed that is seriously threatening the survival of a species that has called earth its home for more than 54 million more years than us homo-sapiens and...

2. Our obsessive need to be in dominion over other beings on this planet. This collective consciousness that has put human life ahead of all other life forms. A strange concept when science is teaching us what the mystics have always shared — life is interconnected — we are all a part of the whole!

CONNECTING THREADS IN STORIES

I have always had a fascination for stories ever since I was a little boy when I was introduced to the made up stories of my dad at bedtime. My teacher, Mrs. Howard, was instrumental in feeding the love of a good tale at junior school and when I found that people enjoyed hearing me tell a tale, I delved into finding more for the telling.

As my volume of world stories increased I was particularly drawn to those of my homeland. Where the so called 'Celts' left a trail of wisdom in myth and folktales. The one great piece in regards to stories is they unite us — another interesting facet is they untie us.

I share this as when I was formulating this segment I originally wrote untie instead of unite. As I went to change the spelling I kept ending up with the word untie! It made me realise that Spirit was asking me to share this two-fold process. Undoubtedly stories unite all races, I have always been intrigued to find a tale from one culture told within another. Basically the same story except for cultural changes in names, places, animal figures, etc. The other thread that Spirit invited me to explore here is the inherent wisdom within the folds of our myths, legends, faerie, and folk tales. When we are willing to delve into the spaces between the spaces of a tale, it helps us untie strands that have kept us stuck in the world. It is in seeing ourselves through the eyes and hearts of all the characters and situations and then in asking ourselves the difficult questions that keys appear to set ourselves free. We have to first do the work needed to shift any undated patterns for ourselves until we become the medicine of the transformation to be found within. It is all about untangling and untying the knots!

The commonalities between the cultural races of human beings that have developed across this globe are shared through exploring our relationship with the many other beings that we share this miraculous planet with. I delighted in finding this following story from Chad in Africa, one that is a familiar to the 'Celtic' world. In this version the leading character is an elephant whereas the 'Celts' would introduce us to a seal!

AN ELEPHANT' SKIN

A young man scouted the banks of Lake Chad looking for the prints of the animals that had visited the area recently. His eyes grew big when he saw Lion paw prints freshly made in the earth. He was on the hunt; however, he wanted to steer clear of the razor sharp claws and teeth of a predator that would quickly make him into the prey. He felt foolish now heading out on his own rather than waiting to join the village hunting party. He had dreamed of bringing home meat for a glorious feast that would set him aside from his peers. He could then claim the hand of a beautiful bride that would be the envy of the other young hunters in his tribe.

He was skittish and the thought of facing a pride of Lions alone had his heart racing. He looked frantically for somewhere to hide. In his fear he dove headlong into the cover of a Tamarisk tree. Instead of landing on the hard earth, he was shocked to feel the thick padding of a neatly folded Elephant's skin beneath his sprawling frame.

His first thought was the Lions had killed it. However, that made no sense for there were no bones. The mystery was compounded by the way that the skin had been packaged up and tucked so carefully away.
As he sat in the shade of the tree trying to decipher how the skin had been so methodically stored, he heard the most beautiful singing voice that had ever graced his ears. It came from the waters of Lake Chad. Peeking through the evergreen leaves, he saw a young woman who looked heavenly to his prying eyes.

She was the prettiest maiden he had ever gazed upon. She was big boned with an ample bosom and he knew that she would be his greatest catch if he could persuade her to marry him. His mind raced with ideas until he formulated a plan. A big grin lit up his face as he came to the conclusion that he was no fool after all. The Elephant skin placed behind the tree may be connected to this young vision of loveliness. Quietly and carefully he lifted the heavy skin and exerting a lot of effort he carried it off and hid it in a secure location. He then raced back and covered his tracks before retreating to hide behind another nearby tree.

He waited, watching patiently, admiring the young woman from his hidden post. He was captivated by her grace and lightness of spirit as she playfully frolicked in the water. She took her time laughing, singing, and splashing merrily in the lake as if in a world of her own. The young man felt like he had entered another realm like he was under an enchanted spell. His heart pounded as she exited the water and stepped nonchalantly towards the Tamarisk tree to retrieve her skin.

He heard a squeal and then a primal scream followed by sobs of tears as the young woman scrambled around desperately searching for the lost skin. She darted from one tree to another hoping that she had been mistaken as to where she had left her prized bundle. As she ran towards the young man's hiding place he stepped out into her path. She pulled up abruptly as he gingerly implored, "Why do you cry beautiful maiden?"

"I am lost. My clothes have disappeared and without them I cannot return to my family. In losing my garments, I will not be able to return to my family, my friends, and I will never be with my loved ones." A steady flow of tears streamed down her cheeks. Her vulnerability brought tears of joy to the hunter's eyes. He had snared her and in her fragile state he would be her saviour, her hero!

As she looked into his misty eyes she mistook his tears for empathy. His voice was gentle and reassuring and she took a small measure of comfort from his words.

"I cannot help you with your clothes or your family, but I can help you discover a good life," cajoled the hunter. "I will fetch you a suit of clothes and I will introduce you to my family." He waited a for a couple of heartbeats before going gently in for the kill, "If you agree to be my wife, I will provide a good life for you. I will cherish any children we will have and I will love you like no other. Your belly will always be full for I am a hunter. And your heart will hopefully open to me as my heart has opened to you," he declared proudly. He smiled victoriously, impressed with how smoothly his words rolled off his tongue. He had struck her with his fine words and dazzling charm and felt confident that his aim was true — she would be his biggest and best catch yet!

The young woman, unknowingly ensnared in his trap, agreed to marry the hunter. His status within the tribe increased exponentially as his exotic wife joined village life. She was well loved by the people for she had an innate wisdom and proved to be skilful at so many of the day to day tasks. She was strong, clever, and resourceful; she was also fertile giving birth to five healthy children: four boys and a girl blessed their union within *the first five years of their marriage. They were all big children and grew to be as strong and as clever as their mother.*

The young woman's voice was remarked on as being soulful, yet all who heard her agreed that there was a melancholy to her song, especially when a herd of elephants came into view. She would often look longingly towards the horizon and at times she seemed so far away as if a daydream had taken her to a different world altogether.

One year there was a famine and the grain store was nearly empty. The husband left the village early one morning with a hunting party. The five children were playing a game and one of the boys chose to hide behind the last sack of grain in the storage hut. To his amazement he found a large leather bundle lodged tightly between the sack and the wall. When the other children bounded in looking for him they found him quizzically examining a large leather skin. When they shared their discovery with their mother she jumped up looking noticeably younger. She raced to the grain store and hugged the skin close to her body.

She gathered her children to her and spoke gently and sincerely, "Children, I love you and I always will. You are all strong and will be the leaders of this tribe one day; you will have large strong offspring whose children's children's children will be leaders too. Your father stole something from me several years ago which you have returned to me. This skin is my true nature and offers me freedom. A chance to return to my kin. If ever you need me sing and I will find you."

The woman then slipped effortlessly into her own skin and walked in glory as an elephant once more returning to the bush.

Her children would sing from time to time and their mother who grew to be the matriarch of her herd would come to them, sometimes in their dreams and sometimes in their waking moments they would see her watching them from the bush. As she prophesised, her children became the ancestral leaders of the clan and they chose a totem — the strong wise elephant!

POWER OF THE TALE

Stories are such great teachers. I wonder which pieces spoke most loudly to you from this tale. The first thing that jumped out when I came across it is how similar in essence it is to some of the Selkie 'Celtic' tales of my homeland.

We have no wild elephants in this part of the world, yet we have a great flair for connecting with magic and mysticism. There are families in the 'Celtic' lands that claim heritage from the seal people — magical Selkies whose skins were left along the shore line while dancing with their clan, stolen by a human who wed them. Wee bairns born and raised until years later the skin is found hidden in a barn and the Selkie is set free. To this day there are families in the British Isles and Ireland who claim their lineage is infused with the blood of the Selkie folk.

The key piece that strikes me from this African tale is how so often humans try to change the nature of another human and other beings that cross their path, including the land itself.

Through sitting with this story we are afforded the opportunity to examine many poignant strands that take us into the shadow and light of our lives.

Where do we look to rob others of their life force and their true nature? It is only in asking ourselves challenging questions and then being authentic with the answers, that we have the opportunity to grow.

Where are we hiding the true nature of our own skin? How comfortable are we being authentic in the skin that we share with the world? Are we being true to our souls calling?

The young woman sings a song of melancholy, although she goes about her tasks and becomes a valuable contributor to the tribe. There are two pieces here for me: 1) How, in the face of adversity, do we still rise above it to be valuable members of society? 2) Where is the song of melancholy stuck within us? I write comprehensively about working with sadness, anger, fear, and all of the attributes that come along with the blockages that result in us stuffing past hurts and trauma into the folds of our bodies through my book — *Magical Crows. Ravens and the Celebration of Death.* These feelings are so important for us to acknowledge and transmute so that we do not walk around in a skin of a life half lived!

The hunter uses his skills to craft a web of deceit. His honey-tongued words are used as a weapon of manipulation that paint a picture of a hero. I wonder where and when are we being taken in by a false prophet, a fake friend? On the shadow side, it is important to examine where we are manipulating others. Where are we pretending to be something we are not to court favour and attain our goal at the expense of others?

It is interesting to note that what we put out comes back to us in the end. The hunter may have gained temporary high status and the admiration of his tribe, yet in the end he loses it all in the discovery of his deeds. Whenever we are out of alignment with Sovereignty, when we look to have dominion over others, it comes at a cost. It may not have the appearance of disaster written over it initially; however, at some point each of us will be effected by our harsh choices just as we are effected by those that offer the highest good to the world.

In this story the hunter's choice impacts his wife's freedom. When she discovers her skin both his and her actions impact their children as they watch their mother fly free.

This raises an interesting question for each of us. I wonder what we would do in the mother's situation? Would we have left our children to walk in the truth of our own skin or stayed by their side?

I know when I divorced many years ago my calling was to leave the USA and return to my native homeland in the British Isles. I waited several years before returning to live in Scotland so I could see my children through high school. I did not want to put them in the situation of having to choose which side of the Atlantic to live on at that time. I did not feel that was fair on them or their mother. I also chose to be close in proximity to them during their transformational teenage years.

Ultimately, I followed my hearts calling to fly home and put my roots into the soil of the land that sings so richly in my heart.

There are so many gems to uncover in the rich tales of the ancestors. I hope you have enjoyed exploring pieces of yourself through some of the questions that the story posed here through me and of course I hope you found some other tasty morsels within the tale for exploring on your own!

STORIES ABOUND

African myths abound with elephant stories. There is a wonderful trickster tail of how Elephant and Hippo were duped into a tug of war against themselves thinking they were actually competing against Hare. Hare is fed up with being called small and weak so weaves a strong rope out of vines and challenges both Elephant and Hippo to a contest of strength. It is Hare's mental strength that wins the day as Elephant and Hippo pull from two different water holes wondering to themselves how come Hare is strong. For hours they tug with all of their might until Hare cuts through the vines leaving both of the pachyderms falling heavily into their respective watering holes.

Another tug of war tale shares how the once short snouted Elephant gains a long trunk in a tussle with Crocodile. Crocodile tries to eat Elephant; however, after a long hard battle tugging and stretching Crocodile lets go leaving Elephant with the nose you see today. Once all of the elephants saw how useful the longer trunk was for foraging and feasting they all visited the watering hole and taunted Crocodile until tug of war after tug of war took place!

Many African elephant tales revolve around anthropomorphizing elephants. There are tribes who claim direct descent from elephants and those who believe past human chiefs and ancestors take an elephant's form in a following life. When the Ashanti of Ghana find a dead elephant in the forest they prepare a proper chief's burial to celebrate their former human leader.

ELEPHANTS AND DEATH

Elephants live in family groupings and when they are separated from a loved one by death or capture the elephants go through a mourning process. Science has recorded some interesting facts that show that elephants grieve their dead. When they encounter the remains of a dead elephant it is not uncommon for the herd to touch the remains of the body with their trunks and the bottoms of their sensitive padded feet. They have been witnessed to stand beside a deceased companion for hours at a time as they caress the fallen body of their kin wrapping their trunks around the tusks of a loved one with empathy and care.

There have even been sightings of elephants attempting to bury the remains of family members by kicking dirt over the skeletons and covering them with palm fronds.

Elephants have been witnessed returning to the grave sites of their kin. It has also been noted how elephant clans have specific burial grounds that they look to help the dying members of their herd return too as long as their death is not sudden and traumatic!

The caution and care that they show when coming across the bones of an elephant that has died along their pathway is heartfelt. It is important to note that they do not show the same kind of interest in the remains of any other species.

UNLAWFUL DEATHS

Elephants are still being killed for the ivory trade with reports of thousands being slaughtered each year. The consequence of poaching drastically affects the herd when an older matriarch is taken. Because elephants increase their memory through age and experience, when an older elephant is taken that information dies with her. With poachers targeting the larger older elephants, herds are left without key knowledge leaving them at a distinct disadvantage.

It is also important to note that female elephants in Africa, alongside their male counterparts, have tusks which attract poachers looking for ivory. Asian elephants vary significantly with not all males having tusks, those without are known as muknas while about fifty percent of female elephants have short tusks known as tushes which are usually no longer than a couple of inches beyond the lip line.

Although the numbers for elephant poaching has decreased for the fifth straight year in Africa, elephant populations are continuing to fall. The new challenge to their survival is an existential one. A fight between humans and wildlife for land, food, and water. A war that to the detriment of elephants, the humans are winning.

This war involves us all, for a farm that was once an ancestral habitat for elephants is contributing to the decline of the world's elephant population. How come you may ask? With the increased expansion of the human population we crave more space on the planet. As humans claim more land for themselves there are less wild habitats for all of the other beings we share the planet with. With more human mouths to feed, more crops are grown. Fully grown elephants on average weigh between 8,000 pounds and 15,000 pounds. When a herd wanders through newly acquired farm land that is part of their ancestral pathway, the farmers are outraged by the damage. This sets up a local war between humans and elephants.

For those further afield it is important to know where our produce comes from. So many beings are mistreated for humans to satisfy their hunger. Our grab and go culture has led us to be desensitized from nature. Whether we are carnivores or herbivores each bite of food we take has an impact on the planet. From air miles to the wellbeing of the land and the beings that have been harvested for our consumption, life has either been cherished or abused. One thing that hit home for me as I researched the impact that land loss is having on elephants, is how important it is to take responsibility for my footprint on the earth. If we get incensed about a poacher's bullet while consuming produce from land that was once an ancestral elephant habitat, we are having just as big an impact upon on the diminishing numbers of elephants upon the planet. Our actions matter!

Of course our responsibility for the planet goes beyond elephant welfare – it asks us to consider the welfare of all creation.

CO-EXISTING

In East Africa the elephant population halved in just a decade while estimates suggest that Africa's human population, which was 477 million in 1980 and now stands at 1.2 billion, is set to double by 2050!

Some serious pause for thought here. There appear to be no easy solutions; however, with all of these statistics and challenges being brought to our consciousness, it calls for us to add our voice to the support of finding ways to co-exist. One idea that was gifted to me by the elephants involves opening ourselves up to once again talking to all of our relations. To put down the gun and to open our hearts to finding both the true meaning of strength and of being homo-sapiens.

"IF WE COULD TALK TO THE ANIMALS — WHAT A NEAT ACHIEVEMENT THAT WOULD BE"

My return journey to an elephant sanctuary in Kerala in 2017 provided an interesting thought provoking conversation between myself and three elephant bulls.

Where I had flown solo four years previously, I now headed with three friends to visit the elephants in the same sanctuary that was recommended by the retreat centre on my previous stay. Driving through the small town towards the sanctuary on a beautiful sunlit day, my thoughts drifted to the only elephant I had witnessed so far on this visit to India. It had been on my very first day as we neared Varkala. A lone handler walked behind a magnificent bull that pounded the scorching tarmac of a busy road in chains. I wondered if he resided in this sanctuary when not being put to work out in a public arena.

The foreboding gates of the sanctuary loomed up ahead. We climbed from the tuk-tuk, pushed open the gates, and entered the harsh prison- like home of several mature elephant bulls. The handlers were sitting idly along the same wall where they had been on my previous visit. Their demeanour was apathetic towards us. Our taxi driver spoke in a local tongue with them and he told us we were not to approach any the elephants directly. We were instructed that we could view them from afar.

I had informed my friends on what they may expect to see —
elephants chained and living in squalid conditions. Walking
through those gates four years previously had been a piercing
blow to my heart. I prepared them as best I could and I knew it
would still be painful to witness the harsh reality that the
elephants were forced to live under each and every day. We
came to bring the elephants a gift of song. The group that I was
with had come to India to celebrate the Crow Festival of
Karkidaka Vavu (see my book *Magical Crows, Ravens and the
Celebration of Death* if you are interested in knowing the details
on this magical journey). They had all worked with me before
and were familiar with the practice of Amrun, the indigenous
song that sings us.

The essence of Amrun is all about getting out of the way and
allowing the song of Spirit to flow through us. I have found it to
be a multi-dimensional tool that supports life in a myriad of
ways.

I had brought the gift of Amrun on my previous visit and it had
been received well. Now as a group, we set a clear intending to
offer this indigenous medicine practice to the elephants before
us. To work the lines of love, hope, and of opening ourselves to
communicating in a deeper way with the elephants that we met
that day.

The first port of call was to check in with the elephants to see if it was okay to bring this gift of song to them. This might sound strange to someone who has not spent a lot of time in wild places listening to the land and the beings that we share this earth with. I have found that all beings have a voice and if we tune in to the energy and communication lines that run between us, it is possible to sense kinaesthetically, visually, or aurally a common language that is shared between all species.

This goes back to the first story where all of the animals once talked to each other. I believe that they never stopped talking to us, we just forgot how to listen. I think it goes further than animals. All life shares stories with us. Many gardeners talk to the plants in their gardens. Why? Because plants respond to words of empowerment. People with 'green fingers' know this. Many of them will also understand at some level that the plants talk to them.

Similarly, many animal lovers know that their dogs, cats, etc. have ways to communicate with them in a definite language that is beyond our common tongue. So we can all tap into a universal language. And I believe the more we practice being present with and connecting with life, the more our intuitive senses open to understand the nuances of all the different species we share this miraculous planet with.

How does the whole 'Dr. Dolittle' approach work — whereby we talk with the animals? I cannot fully answer that. I have pondered it. Is it me speaking through the elephant, the elephant speaking through me, or is the elephant directly talking to me with me responding through words and/or a telepathic conversation? I am unable to give an accurate answer; however, verbal and non-verbal communication takes place to a point whereby I feel the conversation, understand it, and trust it implicitly. If this is something that you cannot get your head around then let go of trying to intellectualise it and instead open your heart to the possibility of it. Perhaps then you will get a glimpse and see, feel, hear, and/or sense whether this truth of mine is also a truth for you.

My experience is that you have to work it for it to work, in fact it goes beyond that — it is ultimately about being the medicine, being absolutely present in the moment, being at one with self so we can be one with others. I return to this truth that many people share — of being connected to all life! If this is a cosmology that resonates in your bones, then you will understand that we are a part of all that is. In other words, I am a single grain of sand, I am a wave on the sea, I am an elephant bound in chains in a sanctuary in Kerala. By being present with another being, I am in essence being present with myself!

When we practice this art, we build muscle and suddenly we are able to understand far more than we ever thought possible. I also trust that in believing that the impossible is possible — *magic happens*. We have the capacity within us to open doorways to the unknown, these mysteries are denied to us while we continue to separate ourselves from nature.

REMEMBERING A KINDNESS

As I stood before three bulls with their magnificent tusks sadly blunted, I sensed not only their permission to weave with Amrun with them, I also sensed recognition.

Research has educated us that elephants have exceptional memories. They use them to great effect for survival, which is why some of them live for sixty plus years in the wild – a figure which is far higher than those kept in captivity.

It has been recorded that elephants remember injuries from those who have hurt them in their lives. So it only makes sense that they remember those who have shown kindness and generosity.

In 1999, workers were enlightened at The Elephant Sanctuary — a non-profit organisation in Tennessee. This sanctuary appears to embody the word for its true meaning. It is a refuge for endangered elephants and one of the largest of its kind in the USA. A new arrival caused quite a stir when she was introduced to one of the elephants already housed in this natural habitat. An elephant by the given name of Jenny became incredibly animated when an elephant that had been named Shirley was brought into the sanctuary. The two of them were so delighted to meet that workers looked into their histories and found that over twenty years earlier the two of them had performed together in the same circus.

This telling evidence shows that it is not only their herd companions that they remember, it is others who have made a strong impression on them. Is it such a stretch for the imagination to see that elephants will also recognise people that they have bonded with even briefly and after several years apart?

For Jenny and Shirley, a surrogate mother and daughter relationship was formed. Jenny had been a mere calf when they had first crossed paths. According to Carol Buckley, Executive Director of the Sanctuary, the strength of their bonding shifted relationships with other elephants who previously had been companions and friends into becoming sisters and aunts.

Jenny was born wild and free in Sumatra. She was captured and stolen away from her homeland in 1973, a year after her birth. It was then she met Shirley for a moment in time, a single winter as she began a twenty-year journey as a circus performer. Jenny was obviously a feisty cow because she ran away from her trainers during circus performances on numerous occasions. She was eventually sent to Illinois for breeding where she sustained a nasty leg injury while being mated with a bull. Her injury was of a serious nature and yet was left untreated leaving her with permanent damage.

She was then declared as unfit for breeding and sold to another circus. Her health deteriorated to the point where she struggled to get in and out of the circus trailer so was left to vegetate inside. She became severely distressed, was malnourished, and was abandoned at a small animal shelter with a degenerative foot disease. The shelter exposed her to a life of being chained up at night time due to a lack of facilities where she stood for hours in her own faeces in freezing cold temperatures.

The silver lining of her life came in 1996 when she was taken to Hohenwald Elephant Sanctuary in Tennessee where she would eventually meet up again with Shirley. She lived another ten years before a hidden bacterial infection from the original untreated injury flared up. Reports from the Sanctuary are that her last days were incredibly touching in the care that Shirley offered to her surrogate daughter. When Jenny finally collapsed Shirley went into mourning and refused to eat for two days.

A winter meeting twenty years previously spawned a deeply meaningful relationship between two these beings.

THAT WHICH MAKES AN IMPRESSION IS REMEMBERED IN THE FLAMES OF THE HEART

Now I fully understand that my interaction with the elephants in 2013 was a fleeting moment in time; however, it had been a powerful meeting of mind, heart, and spirit. The elephants had left a huge impression on me and perhaps I on them. Returning felt like a reconnection. As the song of Amrun passed through my bones I felt my heart opening wider and a deep rich conversation passed between three captive bull elephants and myself.

My three other friends joined me in front of a tiny enclosure that had a tin roof offering these three bulls some protection from the scorching sunlight.

BOUND IN CHAINS

The first elephant was chained by one leg as was the third, the second elephant was chained by three of his legs. None of them could take a step forward as all three of them were tethered to concrete posts. I felt their anger and their frustration at being bound in this way.

Each of them was subjected to standing on a hard concrete floor. I have mentioned earlier how sensitive an elephant's feet are. Standing for hours on end on an unnatural surface while being chained in this way is painful and cruel.

WALKING THE TALK

An amazing fact that I found whilst researching elephants is how they communicate seismically. It is through earth vibrations that messages are sent from one elephant to another. With vocal chords eight times the size of humans, elephants emit two types of sound waves. A high frequency vibration can be heard in a more common fashion using their ears, this sound travels quickly through the air for short distances up to around one mile. However, low frequency waves that rumble through the earth can travel up to six miles away. When an elephant feels the earth reverberate in this way they press their heavily padded foot onto the earth. They have dozens of touch receptors on this pad which send signals to their brain.

Research has shown that if a warning cry is sent using the high frequency method elephants receiving this message through their ears will take immediate measures to protect themselves. If the message is sent via the low frequency method the elephants acknowledge it and are less perturbed as they know danger is still quite some way off.

Other really interesting facts that I gleaned in regards to elephant communication is that their understanding of syntax suggests that they have their own language and grammar. Elephants have not only wonderful artistic abilities in being able to combine colours and elements, intriguingly they are incredibly musical. Research has shown that they recognise twelve distinct musical tones and they can recreate melodies.

The song of Amrun is multi-dimensional. I have worked with people weaving with the threads of this language into all of the elements, earth, air, fire, and water, while simultaneously being the Amrun of these elements. What does this mean? Well simply I become the vibration of whichever element I am working with — for example, water. As the song of water sings through my body I become the flow of water. This is an indigenous way, what shamans and medicine people have worked with for eons.

As well as the elements, I have also sung other aspects of Amrun into my three bodies and into the bodies of other beings. Through this practice I have become the threads of love, peace, joy, and an array of emotional strengths to support the intending of the healing process I am working with.

There are so many things that we do not fully comprehend in the world and it is easy to dismiss something that is not part of our everyday understanding as "weird," "rubbish," or "poppycock" — we humans are quick to dismiss that which we don't understand.

I don't know if the elephants received the messages I was sharing through Amrun via their feet, their ears, their eyes, their smell, other senses or a combination of all of these; what I do know is that the interaction between us was real and incredibly clear.

The first elephant pointed with his trunk to my three friends and then to me and he became incredibly playful. I felt his whole demeanour change, the anger and frustration dissipated, he became joyful, and had the most amazing smile upon his face. Research confirms that elephants are capable of deep thought and complex feelings.

I felt his joy and through this focused playful interaction a deep communication took place.

THE PHYSICAL BODY

He had once known freedom in the wild; he missed the soft earth under his feet. Physically he was trapped and he yearned to be free once more. Yet the song gave him hope. I sensed he felt freedom beyond his physical body and as he relaxed into the waves of Amrun, this fabulous bull and I entered into a sacred dance together. When the last notes of expression flowed from my lips, this colossal being stood before me in a very different way. He was lighter, brighter and so was I.

My communication receptors were opened up and I received thoughts and feelings that connected to the freedom of the physical body. Questions flowed through me. Where do we humans trample so hard on the earth, stomping our feet in our demands to be right and get our own way when essentially we are going nowhere? We have tethered ourselves to concrete that flows onto the earth coating the fertile softness of living flesh with an unyielding coat that looks to suppress and suffocate. Our increasing network of roads and buildings sprawl unceasingly over land that was once forested and thriving with wildlife. So many humans engaging in ripping up flesh in their own back yards in a desperate attempt to manicure a perfect patch of 'weed' free grass. As my partner Joyce is apt to remind people there is no such things as weeds, only different species of plant life!

I was a young boy in the early 1970's when I witnessed our neighbour pulling plants, bushes, and a small tree from their front garden to lay a concrete patio for the sake of convenience. This trend of coating the soil has grown with those who do not want the responsibility of working with a small patch of earth — nurturing the soil and the plants that grow within it. And some humans lay down synthetic grass — an artificial turf for that perfect looking lawn!

Many others who do keep their lawns look to manipulate them in such a harsh way with poisons and non-indigenous plant life which does not support the indigenous wildlife. Style over substance, ease over a daily connection to life. This leads many to retreat into their concrete bunkers. I witness so many humans shutting themselves away from nature creating luxurious prisons that ultimately separate themselves from their true nature.

My observation of elephants being stripped of their freedom reminds me of the bullying aspect that adults condemned when I was at school. In early childhood education we are taught to share, that being spiteful to others talking behind their backs, and causing another pain is simply wrong. Yet the playground antics of the bully are carried into adult life with a fervour. Why? Well, the children look to the adults who are mouthing words about being 'nice' while their actions demonstrate patterns of destruction. Oppression is rampant in many families, local communities, social media, and religious organizations, from the factory floor to the corporate boardroom and the so called 'members' and 'leaders' of governments around the globe. While many journalists and newshounds feed the fear factor while promoting 'witch' hunts in the name of entertainment.

As a side note I am called to say that as a society we have given the name 'witch' a bad rap! I address this in "Magical Crows…" For now, let me stay with the hypocrisy of our childhood teachings.

So much of what we are taught in our formative years of education is tossed to the wind as we trample over each other in a desperate conquest to win, to be better than others. This highly competitive nature feeds society with feelings of unworthiness. It is the hungry ghost syndrome where enough is never enough! An expression that is used to justify this winning mentality is 'survival of the fittest.'

TEACHINGS OF THE BULLY FROM THE BULL

As I held eye contact and an energetic physical heart connection with the first elephant, my understanding the role of the bully came flooding through. The only reason we put another being down is because in that moment we feel unworthy, unloved. Our need to make others look, seem, and feel small is so that we can look, seem, and feel better and bigger about our own life. Bullies ply their trade using fear tactics and yet at the heart of it they are afraid. In their demonstration of strength, they are actually showing weakness. And yet this illusion is difficult to comprehend for the being who is experiencing the oppression. It is incredibly challenging for some witnesses who can find themselves clasped in chains if they stand up to a bully who is backed by the laws of the land.

Many ethnic minorities know this feeling as do many women, transsexuals, lesbians, and gay men. It is all too easy to point the finger at the white male race and though the Caucasian male has a lot to answer for, as does the patriarchal world in general, the act of bullying has seeped into the human psyche and has become an accepted aspect of life on Earth. We rally and shout from time to time against the oppressors and yet this age old art of abuse continues to thrive in the world on so many levels.

As I stood before the three chained elephants, the message to stand strong in the physical world and to end self-inflicted oppression came bubbling to the surface. The elephant chained to the post was asking me to begin with myself, inviting me to have the courage to increase strength and freedom in my physical body and to bring this wisdom to the masses. If each of us humans break the chains that exist between our physical bodies and our mental state, we will liberate ourselves. In this thought I felt a ray of hope flash between us. As if our wellbeing will affect the wellbeing of others. As if the fate of our very existence was bound together.

There was an acknowledgement between this wise pachyderm and my heart that the other two bulls chained up in this enclosure represented aspects of the other two bodies — the mental body and spiritual body. That my communication with them would open me up to revelations about these other two bodies that are part of wholeness, oneness — physical, mental, and spiritual health.

THE MENTAL BODY

The second elephant was bound three times to the concrete post. He was the most agitated of these three elephants being held against their will. Not only did I work with him with the song of Amrun, the first elephant whose energy had shifted to a playful and joyful state joined in comforting the frustrated bull.

Dr. Joshua Plotnik and renowned animal behaviour expert Frans de Waal shared findings in regards to elephant empathy. Elephants consistently demonstrated an ability to console their kin. In a yearlong study of twenty-six Asian elephants in a Nature Park in Thailand they witnessed elephants rushing to the side of a distressed companion and chirping softly, stroking the head and genitals of the upset elephant, even placing their trunks into the others mouth, which is a huge sign of trust because of the risk of being bitten.

The first elephant offered soft chirps to the song that sang through me and stroked the distressed elephant.

This second one, who I will refer to as the *wisdom of the mental body,* began slowly to relax. I heard him clearly ask me to break his chains, to set him free. I felt tears flowing down my cheeks as I held his gaze. I explained that it was not in my power to physically set him free in that moment. I shared how us humans have got stuck in our heads. That the Patriarchal world is being led from a distorted understanding of what drives our thoughts in this world.

I discovered several years ago that our 'Celtic' ancestors had a belief system of three cauldrons, energy centres, in our bodies. The head being the cauldron of knowledge, the pelvis being the cauldron of warming, and the heart being the cauldron of calling or vocation. It was the heart and not the head that was deemed to be the thinking centre!

Somewhere along the pathway of life we shifted perspective and in the Patriarchal world most men seem to think either with the brains in their head or the heads of their penis!
As I connected to this being who symbolised the wisdom of the mental body, he grabbed the chain around his neck with his trunk and pulled it into his mouth. I heard his thoughts as clear as daylight. "Humans are stuck, it is time to break the chains that enslave you, it is time to free your minds."

I told him that I agreed whole heartedly. I shared that slowly and surely we are waking up. I hope that enough of us will awaken in time. I told him that my understanding is that for the evolution of our species to take effect it will require the masses to get out of our heads and into our hearts. To find the bridge that connects everything below and everything above us to everything inside of us. When our sexuality, the cauldron of warming, and our great source of knowledge, the cauldron of our brain, is harnessed in the chamber of our heart, we will see, think, hear, feel, and sense ourselves more clearly. When we bring the capacity to love ourselves unconditionally to the world, we will recognise ourselves in all beings and in so doing, we will dance with all species in a very different way. I told him I have hope that both the human race and the elephants of the world will free ourselves from our current road toward possible extinction!

Extinction! — This might sound dramatic and yet the recent population boom, alongside the estimated growth of the human population forecast over the next few years, points towards a serious threat to the elephants' survival on this planet. The facts are that their grazing lands are being stripped from them and developed into human habitats.

With our fervour for putting the humans ahead of all other life forms, I wonder how long the Earth will tolerate us? If our over reliance on technology crashes, we would face incredible hardships. We do not have an inherent right to be here and though humans and elephants are on different sides of the numbers, I feel we are closer to vanishing from the Earth plane than most people think. A case of too many and too few leading to disastrous consequences for all.

We have seen wolves, bears, and reindeer, amongst other native species, disappear from the British Isles and Ireland. These beings may exist in other lands yet my homeland no longer witnesses their majesty upon our shores! We have seen too many species driven from their ancestral lands. It is crazy to think that centuries after our ancestors began the construction of temples like Stonehenge and Newgrange, the woolly mammoth, that survived the ice age, was hunted to extinction around 1650 BCE.

If we accept that the Earth is a living being whose land masses and waters are being poisoned at an alarming rate, then surely at some point the bacteria that is causing such disease will be targeted with a vaccine to eliminate the problem. I urge us all to 'wake up' and choose to be part of the solution rather than a continuation of the problem. What is the solution? I believe a huge piece lies within being in sovereignty with all life and firing up the chambers of our hearts!

THE SPIRITUAL BODY

My focus shifted to the third elephant bound and tethered inside the shack; however, the elephant representing the mental body had one last piece of wisdom for me to hear. He picked up coconut husks that were strewn around his feet and launched them up into the air. They pinged off the underside of the tin roof landing upon his head. I heard his words distinctly ringing in my ears, "Until humans get out of their heads and into their hearts the wounds within all three of our bodies will not be fully healed."

The third elephant was exceptionally tranquil. His presence and gentle strength connected me to his huge heart. As we connected I was reminded of the three wise kings who came to witness a birth. He was the third king and he had a question to ask me, one that required an oath. These three wise pachyderm kings had a story to tell and I was a vehicle to share their thoughts. He asked me to swear that I would be a hollow bone that they could talk through.

The song of Amrun flowed between us and I was cognizant of three crows that flew into perch on the rafters above his head. My primary reason for being in India that year was in attending the 'Crow Festival' of Karkidaku Vavu which led to the writing of *Magical Crows, Ravens and the Celebration of Death*. Three is a powerhouse number in the 'Celtic' world, as is five. These three represented the aspects of life-death-rebirth, the physical-mental-spiritual as well as the three aspects of the Morrighan, the 'Celtic' goddess of war who also represents Sovereignty — The divine feminine.

As I pondered the significance of their arrival, two more crows flew into the shelter above the first elephant representing the physical body. These two framed the elephants alongside their three crow sisters. The message that they spoke to me were that they represented the divine masculine like the ravens that accompany Odin — Huginn and Muninn. The memory and thoughts of holding space for the coming together of the masculine and feminine to bring a transformation of the wounded wasteland to a thriving kingdom — where the Queen and King of hearts dance side by side.

Five is the number that represents Sovereignty and adding the number of the crows to the three elephants made the number eight — which represents infinity. Finally, the four humans, Pat, Ryan, Christy, and myself, the four singers of Amrun, were added to the equation. This equalled a total of twelve! Another powerhouse number — twelve disciples, twelve knights of the roundtable, twelve months of the year, twelve signs of the zodiac, twelve-year cycle in Asia and the list goes on...

I was then reminded to take the numbers in twelve, one and two, and add them together to make three. The message of the wise spiritual body, the third elephant, was crisp and clear, "We three species represent all life in this moment. Crows, elephants, and humans. Sovereignty for all beings, balance of the goddess and god energy within us all. Where five makes eight makes twelve makes three makes one. The healing of the physical, mental, and spiritual. These three species combined makes one — all connected to the universal flow of life — oneness!" The third elephant, the representation of the spiritual body, took his trunk into his mouth and flicked saliva into my face, on my mouth, my throat. We looked into each other's eyes, each other's hearts, with a smile beaming between us, I felt the rich blessing of his spit, his DNA, his oath joining mine, a bond that united us as brothers. His spit to lubricate my voice to support the writing of this book. *Magical Elephants and the Wisdom of Strength* is the birth that he spoke of and through the words scribed on these pages, the oath I made that day has been upheld!

Now we pray on a much bigger birth. The birth of the evolution of the human species. A birth that will shape the resurgence of the elephant population if we are brave enough to meet ourselves and stand as the high queen and high king in the sanctuary, the altar of our own hearts!

I find it interesting that the four humans that gathered that day spanned five generations with our elder in her seventies and the youngest member in his twenties. We also represented a balance of the masculine and feminine. We stood as a diverse group — a heterosexual mother and father, a gay man, and a lesbian. All from different family lines, from different parts of the world, yet united by our hearts!

I left the sanctuary with a flame of hope shining brightly within me. I left also with a commitment to share the story of these three bull elephants. Yet there was to be an exclamation point gifted to me later in my journey from the elephants. It came from elephants that had what these three males had once known — the freedom of wandering the land. Elephants within the Mudumalai and Bandipur National Parks were yet to have their say!

ALL CHANGE

My good friend Pat Beck and I took the toy train from Coonor up Ooty passing through other tea plantations with silver oaks flourishing on the land. We were headed towards the Mudumalai National Park. I had stayed there in 1987 when the tourist trade was a sliver of what it is today.

There has been a boom in the amount of traffic: both Indian tourists and those from overseas. Whereby I had stayed in the thick of the forest in a humble shack surrounded by deer and monkeys, villages have grown into towns where hotels and resorts are ten a penny; their prices have sky rocketed as they combine lodging with jeep safaris to see one of India's dwindling wild habitats.

Trying to pick a place to stay was a challenge. I struggled with poor internet signals both whilst in Kerala and then on the road from Varkala towards Mudumalai. I eventually picked a place based on the fact that the resort owner got back to me and on the surface looked to offer a great deal.

On arrival I was disappointed in my choice. However, Pat and I were excited to head out pre-dawn into the forest to experience possible wildlife that may cross our trail.

In 1987, I was not aware of the cruel treatments towards elephants and I had climbed with other tourists onto a platform secured safely on the back of one that had been placed in servitude. It is amazing how blindly we can wander through our lives. As awake as I feel I am, I still blunder my way through certain chapters of my life!

On this occasion we opted to go on a four-wheel off-road safari into the forest that initially proved to be challenging, though it ultimately blessed us with a rich and rewarding experience.

The owner of the resort jumped aboard with a young driver in the front and Pat and I sat in the back. We left the main road and were soon driving through designated routes taking us deeper into the forest.

We came across a herd of deer early in our exploration. Then the driver started to drive in a fashion that verged on being reckless. He was chatting on his phone while roaring up the steepest hills, zipping and spinning the vehicle as if we were at a motor cross rally.

If you have ever been in India and experienced driving on the main roads, then you will know it can be a crazy experience. The constant tooting of horns and the mad dash from lane to lane, swerving past cows in the road, sometimes six to eight vehicles wide on a four lane road. Motorbikes with six people aboard all without helmets on. Organised chaos to my Western eyes. As extreme as the driving had been, this was the craziest. Pat and I were hanging on for dear life as we were bounced around during this manic spell.

The speed and demeanour of the driving took us not only by surprise, it took our breath away. Before we were able to find a voice to put towards our concerns, the young man drove into some thick deep mud and we came to a sudden stop.

STUCK IN THE MUD

He then revved on the accelerator and the tyres spun furiously sinking the jeep further into the quagmire until we were well and truly stuck.

We then sat and waited for a rescue vehicle. We were in the betwixt and between and though advised not to wander too far away from the vehicle, which we adhered to, Pat and I did step out to admire the glorious view.

Another jeep eventually arrived full of Indian men who were also on tour. They were packed like sardines into their vehicle. Nine of them piled out and put their backs into pushing our jeep out of the mire.

It was a good job that the jeeps then followed each other, for within a few minutes our driver, who was busy chatting to someone on his phone, drifted into another messy bog. Again we needed rocking and pushing until some traction was gained and we were able to move along our way.

By now the sun was rising higher and according to our host, our time was nearly up. Before we returned to the road we stopped by a bunch of bones and the remnants of a weathered skin. There before us was the skull of an elephant. A large cow had fallen and her remains had been pecked clean. I wondered how she had died and how long her body had lain there decomposing. I felt an urge to get out of the vehicle to rattle and sing her home; however, I did not follow my heart. I waited too long and the moment disappeared as the vehicle sped away.

FINDING THE STRENGTH TO SPEAK MY TRUTH

My failure to own my voice heightened my disappointment of our trek into the forest. We had spent most of the morning stuck in the mud. To add insult to injury the owner of our resort, who had ridden up front, had completely ignored Pat throughout our journey. He had engaged in conversation with me at points, yet he had even ignored her when she asked a question. The recklessness of our driver and his lack of attention to us as opposed to his phone brought the reality that we had spent most of the morning spinning our wheels crashing in upon us. We trudged to our cabin in low spirits.

We felt let down by the resort owner who had promised so much. To begin with, our off-road safari was billed as a three to a three-and-a-half-hour trip – we only got two and a half! On top of that, I felt like I had let myself and the deceased elephant down. I felt a sense of redemption though when our host came sauntering over with a huge smile on his face and enquired when we wanted to book our next excursion into the forest.

I faced him in Battle Truth rather than splattering him with War Rage. My first words were, "Let's talk about this one first!" I then made him wait, as we had waited in the mud, until Pat and I had poured ourselves a cup of tea. I calmly owned my voice and shared my disappointments, starting with how Pat had been ignored and treated like a second-class citizen. I honoured that we come from different cultures; however, as a host working with Westerners who pay top rupee for accommodation and excursions it is important to treat women respectfully and as equals to men.

I continued with his choice of driver, who was obviously not up to the task. Getting stuck twice, driving dangerously, and being more interested in his phone, talking to friends and taking selfies, than the task at hand — was simply unacceptable. I know that there was no guarantee that would see wildlife; however, the price we had paid was for the promise of a service that was not delivered. I told him that I lead pilgrimages in the UK and Ireland and I know what it is to give and receive value for money and to provide top-notch customer service. I then gave him an opportunity to make amends. The good news was we were still going to be there for another day. He had time to make it right. My suggestion was that he found a driver that was 100% committed to his task and that he pay the costs for us to go out again that evening for an on-road safari.

Whether it was the fear of a bad review on Trip Advisor or recognition that the morning had been a disaster from his side of things I cannot say, what I do know is that his attitude towards speaking with Pat changed instantaneously. He apologised profusely and agreed to arrange a complimentary evening excursion.

TIME IS NOT LINEAR

Pat and I went for nap and on awakening I felt the call of the deceased elephant to journey to her. As I entered non-ordinary reality the elephant was waiting for me with a clear and concise message.

She advised me to be fully present in the moment, especially when death presents its face for I can honour the transition fully. I have the tools and knowledge to do this. She encouraged me to own my voice and be in the centre of my story rather than be sucked into someone else's.

She took me to being stuck in the mud and I saw it was the young man's story, his poor decisions had lodged us there, my story was what I did with it. Elephant then directed my attention to a troop of monkeys and reminded me I was in control of my own mind. When I got caught up in fear and started spinning out, when I supressed my voice and ignored my intuition, my monkey mind would have a field day. She then took me to her sun bleached bones and looked intently into my eyes and she affirmed that she knew that I knew what to do. I had gone on this trek and given my power away. I had become a tourist. I knew to stop the jeep, to get off and to sing her home, to make offerings and bring the true nature of myself to honour all life.

She spoke with strength and passion, sharing that time is not linear and I had not missed my opportunity to sing her home. Within the journey I was given an opportunity and space to help her cross the rainbow bridge. Seeing her celebrated as she made her way home was an incredibly special gift. I returned to ordinary reality feeling clear, enthused, and totally empowered. I then took offerings down to the stream and rattled while the song of Amrun sang through me.

CHALK AND CHEESE

Our driver arrived early and wow, what a delightful man to cross paths with! We were introduced to a real gentleman by the name of George. I later looked up the meaning of the name and one that I found was 'of the soil' — it fitted him to a tee. He is a retired telecommunications worker who has exceptional communication skills, loves nature, the animals, and has a real zest for life. He sparkled and there was a definite twinkle in his eye. He was born locally and was thrilled to hear that I had visited in 1987 when the landscape was much more tranquil. We reminisced about the pre-tourist boom as we took the main road, a twisting and winding trail that heads through Tamil Nadu towards Bandipur and Karnataka.

We hadn't traversed far before we saw two cow elephants and a calf. I had tears in my eyes as we stopped and watched these amazing beings foraging amongst the trees. They slowly wandered past us within thirty feet of our jeep. If George had turned the vehicle around and headed back to base camp, right there and then, I would have been happy. It felt liberating to see elephants roaming free. And how special to see new life, the little one that was tucked close to its mother was the icing on the cake.

It really felt like they came to see us rather than we went to see them. I remember thinking — everything has changed because we have changed. No longer tourists, we were witnesses. I had been taught a wondrous 'one-drous' lesson: my journey with the elephant had reconnected me to my roots of making love with the land. I had stood up in Battle Truth, I had stood up for the divine feminine. In singing the elephant home, I saw integrity and authenticity being reflected towards me in the shape of these intelligent beings.

After this we saw elephants galore including a large tusked male who was with a sizeable herd. Along with the elephants, we were visited by spotted deer, samba deer, bison, wild boar, several peacocks, and an eagle.

George drove us all of the way to the border of Karnataka before taking us back to the lodge for a final night's stay. Before we reached the town, on the edge of the forest, we were gifted with one last sighting. A mother and baby elephant came out of a thicket and stepped onto the road behind us. George slowed down so that we went at their pace. My thoughts drifted to the first elephant that I had seen, a male in chains on the baking hot hard-surfaced road in Kerala. Now on another tarmac road stepped a cow and calf who were free to roam to the border of the forest land. My prayers were that their grazing lands do not diminish any more than they have already. That a wild space will always be available for them and their descendants to roam free.

We returned to a delicious meal; even the quality of the food had shifted since we spoke our truth or maybe it was just that everything tasted more fragrant with a heart overflowing with joy. Pat and I expressed that we both felt full!

AN EXCLAMATION POINT

The following day we left around the same time that we had with George and we took exactly the same route through Mudumalai National Park to Bandipur and then on up to Mysore. This afforded us an opportunity to say farewell to any wildlife that showed themselves as we journeyed on towards

Chennai. Remarkably, all of the species from the day before were abundantly on display except for elephants. I saw only one single female elephant in Mudumalai. It struck me that I had never seen a single cow on her own in the wild before. I wondered how normal that was. All of my subsequent research talks of females in herds rather than being solitary.

As we reached the border of Mudumalai and Bandipur, Pat and I again saw a single cow. Now my curiosity well and truly peeked. I felt for certain that a third cow would cross our path. To my delight she appeared just before we left Bandipur National Park.

I felt the understanding building way before the third elephant came into view. The strands connecting me to these three strong wise cows connected me to the three majestic bulls that were under lock and key, harshly chained to posts in a sanctuary in Kerala.

As my eyes took in the third wise queen I felt my three bodies stir. Voices of the elephant clan spoke a message — one that carried the true meaning of strength to my heart. A truth that resonated in my bones as it sang through theirs:

"These three cows have the appearance of freedom yet the patriarchal world hems them in. Their ancestral grounds have

shrunk, their male counterparts stolen, like the land, for profit and gain. The abducted bulls bound in chains waiting for their captors to wake up. For the feminine to be truly free the masculine must also be free. To give elephants Sovereignty, humans will liberate themselves. By offering Sovereignty to your own heart you will open a doorway to offering Sovereignty to all beings. Your mind is your heart and the bridge to actualizing the vision of the balance of the feminine and masculine. Your heart matters, you see us, you feel us, we are you, we are one."

FINAL REFLECTIONS

Sometimes I feel the truth of these words as a foreseeable vision. One where we have the strength to evolve into something far greater than what we have been and what we are now. At other times the wave of despair, fear, anger, and hopelessness raises its head and clouds my mind, forcing it to flee my heart space and lodge once more into the familiar pattern of being in my head.

With so many humans rejecting themselves so that they jump easily into rejecting others, with such a deep seated pattern of greed — where enough is never enough — the task of being in Sovereignty with all beings seems so far away.

So when the grey clouds swirl and darken the sky, when despair of being our greatest vision looks beyond the horizon, I invite us all to light a candle of hope in our hearts. I have always been fascinated by words, how in this case the word — *Impossible* — transforms its meaning completely with the addition of an apostrophe and a space. How does this work? Well first let me say that I liken the apostrophe to a ray of hope and the space I equate to a shift in perspective. I also want to point to the importance of each of us taking responsibility for being the change in the world, for investing in our own evolution. For when enough of us believe in the possibility of Sovereignty for all beings, I believe we will activate the shift where *Impossible* becomes *I'm possible*!

As I submitted this final chapter to my editor, my partner Joyce came through to share that there was a report on the radio that two more elephants had just been killed on the railway tracks in India, with authorities promising to look into it. We say that elephants are a protected species, yet their numbers continue to dwindle each year. Until we honour their ancestral grounds our words lack truth.

What I know to be true in my heart is the teaching from the elephants of the true meaning of strength begins in each and every one of us. Waking up to taking responsibility for our own life stories takes courage. As does being present and being willing to open up to a way of communicating with all of our relations in ways that far exceed what we have experienced to date.

As science has gleaned facts to show that elephants exhibit self-awareness through their ability to recognise their own reflection in a mirror, perhaps it is time for us humans to demonstrate self-awareness by seeing ourselves clearly. I believe it is time to honour the true meaning of strength, own our intelligence, and be the ones we claim we have been waiting for.